A
BIODYNAMIC FARM
For Growing Wholesome Food

A
BIODYNAMIC FARM
For Growing Wholesome Food

Hugh Lovel

Acres U.S.A.
Austin, Texas

A
BIODYNAMIC FARM
For Growing Wholesome Food

Printed in the United States of America

Acres U.S.A.
P.O. Box 91299, Austin, Texas 78709 U.S.A.
phone (512) 892-4400 • fax (512) 892-4448
info@acresusa.com • www.acresusa.com

Publisher's Cataloging-in-Publication

Lovel, Hugh
A biodynamic farm for growing wholesome food /
    Hugh Lovel — 1st ed.
    viii, 216 p., 23 cm.
    Includes index.
    Library of Congress Catalog Card Number: 93-74953
    ISBN: 978-0-911311-45-7
    1. Organic farming. 2. Agricultural ecology. I. Title.

     S605.5.L68 2000   631.5'84
                                   QBI00-232

*Dedicated to the proposition
that all biodynamic farms are equally unique.*

Table of Contents

DREAMS

When from life's sordid paths with
      Eager choice
We turn to follow an eternal voice
      That sings
Of beauty evermore
      The wings
On which we soar
      Are dreams of other things.

And though the road be rough,
      The wayside bleak,
Yet in that dreary waste we ever seek
      For themes
On which to fashion song
      It seems
Days aren't so long
      If only we have dreams.

—Isabel Lovel

Glossary

The glossary is in the beginning of this book in the hopes that readers will look through and get definitions of unfamiliar terms before reading the text. Intended definitions of words such as astral, ether and freedom are not found in current dictionaries. Additionally, some definitions are provided to save the reader from referring to dictionaries.

Acre--A field of tillable or pasturable land. A unit of land measure, originally the area plowed by a yoke of oxen in a day, hence a variable unit. The official English (and U.S.) statute acre is 160 square rods, 4,840 square yards, 43,560 square feet or 4,047 square meters. Not to be confused with a hectare, which is 2.471 acres. (See hectare)

Acres U.S.A.--A monthly American farm publication devoted to examining all issues scientific, political or economic as they pertain to the development and implementation of ecological methods of agriculture. "A voice for eco-agriculture."

Aerobic--Able to live, grow, work or take place where free oxygen is present, as aerobic bacteria thrive in a well-aerated soil.

Anaerobic--Able to live, grow, work or take place in the absence of free oxygen, as with anaerobic bacteria in anaerobic soil conditions, which are usually tight, compacted, and/or water-logged, and thus deprived of oxygen.

Agriculture course (Steiner)--Rudolf Steiner's eight lectures on agriculture, delivered in 1924 in German and transcribed for publication from stenographers' notes. An English translation by George Adams was first published in a limited edition in England in 1958. A new American translation by Malcolm Gardner, made for publication in 1994, will contain explanatory footnotes as well as Steiner's written notes and outlines.

Agricultural individuality--Usually this refers to a single biodynamic farm, though it can refer to any farm or closely knit farm community operating as a single entity. A whole farm or farm enterprise and all it comprises, including the farmer, his co-workers, supporters, resources, hopes and abilities.

Anthroposophical cookery--The art of preparing food taking into account the significance of the different parts of the plant--fruit, root, flower and leaf--as they relate to the development of the human organism with its physical head, heart and guts and spiritual thought, emotion and will. It also considers the importance of various localities, seasons, rhythms and species as well as various methods of preparation, combination, processing, refinement, fermentation, and cooking, both for individual health and for human evolution. What, for instance, is the significance of the potato and the tomato, and what does it mean that the sources of most bulk sugars today are the stalks of plants? Why is this different from root sugars or fruit sugars? Why eat some foods raw or others fried? What makes arrowroot powder different nutritionally from corn starch? What is the special significance of milk or honey? Why should a land flowing with milk and honey be thought blessed? Above all, anthroposophical cookery is the art of taking a hand in our own evolution by choosing different foods, prepared in various ways and combinations.

Anthroposophical society--Used here to refer to any, or all collectively, of the societies devoted to furthering the study of human wisdom or spiritual science particularly along lines laid forth by Rudolf Steiner.

Anthroposophy--A study of the wisdom of humanity. This includes but is not limited to the contributions of Rudolf Steiner. It was Steiner's contention that others working from the premises presented in*The Philosophy of Freedom* would arrive at many of the viewpoints he advanced in his life's work, if not much more besides. Anthroposophy sometimes is referred to as spiritual science.

Ares-- The Greek god of war, son of Zeus. Also metric units of land measure equal to 100 square meters or one hundredth of a hectare.

Astral--Of or pertaining to the stars. The astral influences come from the surrounding regions of space, with nitrogen as their vehicle. Astrality works through the nerves and senses and relates to hopes and dreams, ideals and motivations, perceptions and purposes, sensations and desires. It is to be distinguished from etheric vitality, or life force, which works through the organs and chakras. Etheric force does not derive from the locality of visible stars, but is associated with the outermost boundary of the universe and its expansive, quickening (counter-gravitational) influence upon matter. Minerals are not alive in the sense of defying the law of increasing entropy. Thus, though etheric force exerts an influence on them, they have no etheric body. Plants reduce entropy and have ether or life bodies. But, despite the influence astrality exerts on them, it does this from without as they have no nerves and therefore no astral bodies. Animals, with their nervous systems and awareness, have both etheric and astral bodies. Humans, who are aware of being aware and can take a conscious role in their further development, have etheric, astral and egoic bodies. (See astral body, ether, ego.)

Astral body--The sense and desire body associated with the nervous system. During sleep this body may separate from the physical and travel widely, connected to the physical body by what is called the silver cord. Most people are unaware of this beyond knowing they have dreamed.

Astrology--A study of the bodies of the solar system, their motions relative to each other against the starry background and how these relate to life on the earth. Astrology is an ancient holistic philosophical system that takes into account all aspects of life on the earth, placing these in the context of the solar system and the stars. The common astrology used in casting horoscopes (zodiacal charts) is tropical astrology, which has twelve zodiacal signs traditionally beginning with Aries and ending with Pisces. It calls the point where the Sun crosses the equator on the first day of spring zero degrees Aries even though this is roughly thirty degrees away from the actual constellation of Aries. Because human culture is cumulative and the influences of an epoch carry through it, this has validity and is in use despite the fact it no longer reflects the true motion of the Sun, Moon and planets relative to the twelve constellations of the ecliptic (the zodiac). During the time of Ptolemy, approximately 130 A.D., the vernal equinox did occur at zero degrees of the constellation Aries. However, over the past two thousand years, due to the Earth's precessional motion, the vernal equinox has traveled backwards through the constellation of Pisces until at present it is entering the constellation of Aquarius. Biodynamic agriculture relies on sidereal astrology which takes this into account. To some extent animals, but particularly plants, are utterly dependent on the sidereal astrological situation.

Astronomy--A science of the stars and other heavenly bodies or phenomena, dealing with their size, distance, composition, relative motion, mass and the like. This is an outgrowth of astrology that deals with measurable phenomena without considering their significance for life on the earth.

Azotobacters--A genus of large rod-shaped or spherical, non-symbiotic bacteria of the family *Nitrobacteriacea*. They fix atmospheric nitrogen in the presence of carbohydrates, especially in the vicinity of plant roots which exude sugars. Ehrenfried Pfeiffer identified fifty four different species of azotobacters in samples of BD 500. Well-made compost also tends to contain high azotobacter populations.

Balance--An equilibrium of forces and/or materials. Also, to bring to an equipoise or equilibrium.

Barrel compost--A special homeopathic compost (Thun recipe) made with cow manure, basalt powder, eggshell and biodynamic preparations. It is potentized and screened, for composting, into a wooden barrel that is four fifths buried, into which the biodynamic compost preparations are inserted. Commonly it is used as a field spray to bring the influences of the compost preparations to farm land. See Chapter XI.

Basalt--One of the primary types of igneous rock underlying the earth's crust or upthrust by volcanic activity. A dark, tough, heavy, paramagnetic, fire-formed rock--rich in a wide variety of minerals and considered, when ground finely, to be an embryonic soil material well suited for renewing exhausted land. It contains a more diverse mixture of minerals than limestones which are richest in calcium (calcitic lime) or calcium and magnesium (dolomitic lime). Basalt (along with its cousin, granite) is considered to be an excellent soil remineralizer. Depending on the soil's needs, basalts, granites and limestones are all good soil remineralizers, especially when applied to leguminous crops or incorporated into composts, as they tend to draw nitrogen into the soil.

Belief--What one thinks is true or real, either physically or spiritually. Though beliefs can be empowering, they may also be limiting. They can amount to prejudices that obstruct learning, since the mind involuntarily rejects information which contradicts previous beliefs. Beliefs can also be subconscious, and two or more beliefs can conflict resulting in counter-intention and mis-emotion. People often say one thing but believe another. Examining one's beliefs in a more or less comprehensive fashion may help to resolve these conflicts. If one's beliefs involve thinking there is, above all, a Creator, divine order or primal cause (expressed or exemplified through whatever agencies) then one's beliefs may be called religious. (See religion.)

Biodynamic agriculture--Also called BD farming, this is a holistic system of agriculture that grew out of the investigations of Rudolf Steiner. It views each farm as a living individual within the living earth and universe. An ideal BD farm is a self-sufficient ecosystem that produces its own composts, seeds, livestock replacements, etc., and operates within the larger context of the district and its make up, the country, the world, and the rhythms and relationships of the solar family against the starry background. A biodynamic farmer grows food for nourishment, not simply to make money, and the spiritual human requires nourishment as much as the physical. Thus the farmer seeks to produce food that supports the whole human being, including the physical, etheric, astral and egoic bodies. In the view of biodynamic agriculture the threefold human organism is composed physically of head, heart and guts, and spiritually of thought, feeling and will. Food must contain adequate materials for physical organization as well as adequate forces for spiritual activity. We may think of food as our medicine, and not simply medicine for our ills--though it may be. Above all it is medicine for our health and evolution. (See anthroposophical cookery.)

Biodynamic preparations--Natural medicines used on the land to impart the forces necessary for a balanced and healthy environment--also called BD preps and numbered from 500 to 508.

BD 500--This is also called horn manure and is made by packing cow horns with bovine manure and burying them a foot or so deep in fertile soil from late fall through early spring. This is a preparation rich in the formative forces associated with the gravitational, or earthly, polarity.

BD 501--This is also called horn silica and is made by packing cow horns with finely ground (see colloidal) quartz and burying them a foot or so deep in a sunny spot from late spring to early fall. This is the counterpart of BD 500, and is used to stimulate those formative forces associated with the levitational, or cosmic, polarity.

BD 502--The first of the composting preps, this is made by packing yarrow flowers into a male elk or deer bladder near the beginning of summer and hanging it roughly eight feet high in the sun until mid to late fall. Then it is buried eight to twelve inches deep in fertile soil until the middle of the next summer. This prep brings sulfur, which the spirit uses to enter into association with matter, into the right relationship with other minerals, especially potassium. In particular, this relates to the excretory/purificatory process associated with Venus.

BD 503--The second compost prep, it is made by stuffing bovine intestines with chamomile flowers and burying these "sausages" eight to twelve inches deep in a humusy spot from mid to late fall through early spring. This prep brings calcium into a healthy relationship with sulfur, and it relates to the digestive/assimilative process associated with Mercury.

BD 504--This compost prep is made by burying a mass of stinging nettle leaves and stems surrounded with peat or something similar (such as well-rotted sawdust) at a depth of eight to twelve inches in good soil from mid summer of one year to late summer of the next year (ensuring a full solar cycle). This prep brings iron and kindred elements into combination with sulfur. It relates to the circulatory/energizing process associated with the Sun.

BD 505--The fourth compost prep, this is made by packing the finely ground outer bark of an oak tree (especially one with deeply lobed leaves such as the English oak of Europe or the white oak of North America, as these divisions of the leaves exemplify the sulfur relationship) into the cranial cavity of a domestic farm animal such as a cow, sheep, goat, horse or pig, and immersing it, from fall through early spring, in a place where water trickles. This prep brings carbon into combination with calcium, and relates to the development of egoic vitality associated with the Moon.

BD 506--This fifth compost prep is made by enclosing a mass of dandelion flowers, usually about the size of a grapefruit, in a casing made from the mesentery (a part of the peritoneum) of a bovine, and burying this eight to twelve inches deep from mid fall through early spring in a fertile location. This brings silica into the right relationship with potassium (and sulfur) and relates to the regulatory/transformative processes associated with Jupiter.

BD 507--The sixth compost prep. It is made by pressing or squeezing the juice out of fresh valerian flowers. This brings phosphorus into the picture and relates to the metabolic/oxidative processes associated with Mars.

BD 508--This final prep tends to balance the six compost preps which preceded it, and can also be added to compost piles. It is made from dried meadow horsetail herb, usually by boiling. It helps sufficient micronutrients become associated with the major nutrient elements, especially silicon (in combination with oxygen), and serves to temper growth during periods of excessive rainfall. It relates to the hardening/energizing forces associated with Saturn.

Biological transmutation--A term popularized by the French scientist, Louis Kervran, from the English translation of his book by that name. It refers to transmutation of elements by living organisms. It is a field of investigation pioneered in the nineteenth century by Baron von Herzeele, and receiving further validation from Rudolf Hauschka, particularly in his book, *The Nature Of Substance*. Although widely acknowledged by biological growers in Europe, it is scorned in American academic circles. Probably if it were well enough understood farmers could quit buying fertilizers. Without using this term, Steiner refers to biological transmutations in his agriculture course, indicating under what conditions certain transmutations occur. Presaging Kervran's work, he refers to transitional elements not yet acknowledged widely by physicists.

Bovine--Any of the genus *Bovidacea*. A cow, ox, bull or calf. Cattle.

Butterfly effect--This refers to minute changes in chaotic systems which result in large scale alterations of the system. In fluid dynamics this is expressed by the dictum that a microscopic change at a point can effect large scale changes in the medium. It explains how homeopathic dilutions powerfully affect living organisms, and how biodynamic preparations profoundly influence a farm. It is called the butterfly effect by weather forecasters as they imagine something so slight as a butterfly flapping its wings one way instead of another can cause major divergence between what is forecast and what actually occurs.

Carbonic acid--An acid of carbon dioxide existing only in combination with water (H_2CO_3), and reacting with calcium(Ca^{++}), magnesium(Mg^{++}) or other positively charged ions to form carbonates. In his agriculture lectures Steiner indicates that carbon dioxide, while within the body, exists in the form of carbonic acid.

Chakras--(From the Sanskrit meaning wheel.) One of the seven circles of energy in the human body, related to functions in the locality of the chakra. The chakras are, in ascending order, 1) the root, 2) the sacral, 3) the solar plexus, 4) the heart, 5) the throat, 6) the brow and 7) the crown chakras, with the energy entering at the root, where the body's material excretion takes place, and reaching fullest unfoldment in the crown at the top of the head.

Chaos--A chasm, gulf or abyss; the void and formless infinite, hence the state of primordial form. Nascent form, resulting from the dissolution of what preceded it. To be distinguished from randomness. In nature chaos prevails. It is the way life functions rather than by our notions of centralization, linearity and entropy.

Chemical--Having to do with the composition, reactions and transformations of substance. Something produced by the science of substance and its transformations, not necessarily having anything to do with life. Also a substance produced by chemical process or used for producing a chemical effect, as in a chemical or the chemicals.

Chemical farming--The commonest modern farming method, based upon the use of chemical salts as fertilizers. If quality results are to be obtained, this is a high art, as biochemists such as Carey Reams have shown. It cannot be adequately addressed in the crude, seat-of-the-pants fashion that is customary. Usually the results are crops of questionable quality which require further, frequently toxic, rescue measures. But, there is money to be made in this. It is well-researched, recommended and advertised by industries, universities, and farm publications which stand to profit from chemical sales. Since in the short term farmers purchase high cost inputs, crop failures can be financially ruinous, reinforcing the toxic rescue agenda. The long-term, hidden costs involve, among other things, destruction of productive land, overall environmental degradation (particularly water quality), and health losses especially for farm workers and consumers.

Chyme--The semifluid mass of partly digested food resulting from the action of the gastric juice, and expelled by the stomach into the duodenum.

Clear--Unobstructed. Free from impairment.

Colloidal--Of or pertaining to a substance that, when dissolved, diffuses slowly or not at all through a membrane--gluelike. Colloids are often gelatinous, as, for example, albumin, gelatin or starch. Also any substance in a state of fine subdivision or dispersion (with particles ranging between 10^{-5} and 10^{-7} cm. in diameter), as with colloidal phosphorus, iron, or silica.

Combine--In farming parlance a machine for harvesting, thrashing and separating grains. The verb, to combine, refers to the use of such a machine.

Compost--A well-digested mixture of organic residues, usually manure, bedding, wood wastes, food wastes, rendering wastes, soil, and/or powdered minerals (such as limestone, phosphate rock, granite, basalt, leonardite, etc.). Compost piles should be well-aerated with a carbon to nitrogen ratio of between 15:1 to 30:1. This usually involves periodically turning a balanced mixture of nitrogen rich components such as manures or rendering wastes and nitrogen poor materials such as wood wastes or shredded leaves. Composts can be further enhanced by addition of soil and/or rock dusts. They may be inoculated with starters such as the Pfeiffer formula (which contains the BD preps) or (see below), or they may be treated with homeopathic medicines such as the BD preps 502 through 507, (also BD 500 and BD 508). Compost is optimum for use when it is broken down to the point it crumbles and has little or no offensive odor. If it is allowed to go past this point and become mineralized it tends to lose its quickening effect on the life ether of the soil (see ether).

CompoStar--An inoculum of microorganisms for compost making developed and produced by Vaclav Petrik and marketed under this name by Fletcher Sims, Jr., a proponent of composting and compost technology. Like the biodynamic preparations, it is beneficial because of its inherent forces rather than simply the microorganisms themselves. It imparts etheric and astral forces to composts, and has many potential applications. (While it is not recommended people have eaten CompoStar.) Can be used homeopathically, radionically and in conjunction with the BD preps.

Control--Originally to check by a duplicate register or account, or to check, test or verify by counter or parallel evidence or experiments, as in "controlled" experiments. Now commonly to exercise directing influence over. This is a matter of degree, as in how much, or what degree of control one exercises. The essence of control is to use precisely as much force as necessary and no more or no less. Its three elements are start, change and stop (initiate, develop, cease). Lack of ability to simultaneously start, change *and* stop implies lack of control, as starting an automobile and getting it going this way and that, but not being able to stop it implies it is out of control. What control means in terms of exercising directing influence over insects, diseases and pests in agriculture needs to be examined. It is propaganda and flagrant euphemism to say one is controlling insects or weeds by assaulting them with toxic chemistry. It would be more honest to admit we will not control insects or weeds until we can get them started and direct their function, as well as eliminate them when they are not needed.

Corona mill--A small, hand operated grist mill of this brand name, manufactured in South America and sold widely throughout the United States.

Cosmic forces--Those influences that emanate from the periphery; centripetal, levitational.

Cosmic Pipe--A radionic device developed by T. Galen Hieronymus that picks up low level energies and broadcasts them throughout the soil. The reagent well allows for various materials, particularly homeopathics, to be included in the broadcast.

Cosmic substance--Silica, silicic acids and their combinations.

Cow--A female bovine.

CSA--An acronym for community supported or consumer sponsored agriculture; a method of farming where the farm grows a wide diversity of foods while the consumers provide support for the farm operation. This implies that the people eating the food know where their food came from, who grew it and more or less how it was grown. It also implies an extremely diversified and relatively self-sufficient, ecological farm operation.

Decoction--An extract made by boiling.

Demeter--The Greek goddess of fruitful soil and of the operations of agriculture.

Demeter certification--Certification of a biodynamically grown product. The purposes of the Demeter certification organization are to educate and to assist in marketing. Demeter certification comes the closest of any organic certification program to encouraging farmers to produce foods of the highest quality rather than simply meeting minimum standards.

Diamagnetic--Having less magnetization than a vacuum; antimagnetic. A diamagnetic material is repelled in the vicinity of a magnet.

Digestive impulses--All that works to break down organic materials into their basic, universal forms so they can be absorbed as nourishment by living organisms. For plants digestion occurs outside the body of the plant. In animals these digestive impulses operate within the animal's body, starting with the selection of what goes into the mouth. Overall the digestive impulses reveal a certain wisdom or intelligence, both in the way nature provides nourishment to plants from the breakdown of previously exhausted organic forms, and in the animal's ability to choose what will or will not be ingested.

Diversity--Variety, difference. As used in this book, it indicates a wide range of many different species and types. Biological diversity is important in maintaining environmental health and fertility, as may be observed from the fact that loss of diversity precedes declining fertility, soil erosion and desertification. Likewise if diversity is restored, increase takes effect. Fertility improves, soils are rebuilt and desertification is reversed. Put another way, broad based cooperation, rather than head to head competition, produces an abundance in nature. (See symbiosis, synergy.)

Dolomite--A type of limestone containing a high proportion of magnesium, commonly as much as one part magnesium to three parts of calcium. Appropriate as a soil remineralizer only where soils are deficient in magnesium. This can best be determined by quantitative soil tests. Probably magnesium levels should not be much less than a twelfth or more than an eighth of calcium levels.

Double digging--A term popularized by Alan Chadwick, referring to a method of bringing air, and thus etheric and astral forces supportive of life and growth, more deeply into the soil than most cultivation techniques. Commonly this is done with a shovel. A bed is marked off and a short row or strip of spadings are dug out at one end to the shovel's depth. Then the layer below is loosened and aerated as much as possible without removal, whereupon an adjacent row of topsoil spadings is turned over onto the loosened subsoil, so the adjacent subsoil layer can be loosened. Thenn the next topsoil layer can be turned over and the subsoil under that loosened, and so on. At the end of the bed the topsoil that initially was removed is used to fill over the last row of loosened subsoil. While this may not be much use on large farms, it is an excellent gardening method.

Dowse--To divine or conjecture from subtle signs. This involves asking a question or stating an intent and then looking impartially for an indication. Commonly dowsing is associated with the use of an instrument such as a pendulum, "L" rods, "Y" rods or rubbing plate. The best dowsers need only detect variations in the pulse or other subtle signs, such as muscle testing techniques. Dowsing is useful in determining things that one does not know by logic or reason but nevertheless may know by feeling, as in dowsing for water, dowsing for a homeopathic remedy or dowsing for a lost object. The quality of intention of the dowser, especially his impartiality and intent to do good for all concerned, greatly influences the accuracy of his dowsing.

Drill--In farming parlance this refers to a machine for making holes or furrows and placing seeds in them. The verb drill indicates an act of (or technique for) planting seeds (with or without machinery) in holes or furrows in this fashion.

Dynamization--The process of potentizing a homeopathic remedy, usually diluted in water, by stirring it intensively. When a vortex is established by stirring clockwise, the direction is reversed and stirring proceeds counterclockwise to establish a new vortex. Each time a new vortex is fully established the direction is reversed until the remedy is potentized. This can take from fifteen or twenty minutes to as much as an hour. (See potentization, succussion, trituration.)

Earthly forces--Those influences that emanate from the center; centrifugal, gravitational.

Earthly substance--Chiefly lime, or calcium and related elements in their various combinations.

Ecliptic--That great circle of the celestial sphere which is the apparent path of the Sun among the stars, or that of Earth as seen from the Sun. This can be thought of as the plane of the Earth's orbit extended to meet the celestial sphere.

Ecology--The study of interrelationships between living organisms and their environment. This is like defining a hurricane as a movement of air. Such a definition by no means conveys the power and complexity of the reality. As with a hurricane, a strong ecology is an extremely rich, powerful and complex anastomosis of organisms, materials, forces and events. Also, as in an ecology, the community of living organisms along with their resources and dynamics in a given locality.

Economic sphere--That portion of society devoted to producing goods and services and exchanging them. This activity begins with the idea and will of those who produce raw materials and reaches full circle with consumption and recycling or disposal of waste.

Economy--The management of income and outgo of a household, locality, district, region or nation. Also, the sum of production arising from nature and consumption returning to nature, including the dynamics of the participants. The national or world economy may be managed more or less in a laissez faire (let do) fashion. This implies a lack of governmental control over industry and business, but says nothing about how industry and business manage things, whether or not in a helpful and productive way for all concerned. Since special interest sectors of the world economy manipulate governments, including the U.S. government, the pretense of political management of the economy is a diversion, a cover-up. The real questions are who is managing, or mismanaging, what and toward what ends. The predominate reality, as far as the world economy today is concerned, is one of shortage rather than abundance--as may be seen in the fact that world money supplies are for the most part based on debt rather than the elaboration of wealth from nature. Production and consumption alike are stimulated by debt. Both end up subservient to trade. Banking and world trade reinforce their position of dominance by manipulating both the political sphere and the significance sphere of education, values and beliefs. This does not lead to a stable economy or a stable society. The world economy cannot be stabilized as long as debt is monetized instead of raw material production, or producers and consumers do not have an equal political say with bankers and traders, or society believes shortage is inevitable rather than abundance.

Educate--To train or develop, school. Not necessarily to inform or instruct though these are included. Education is a process of awakening knowledge, skill and understanding, which is not necessarily the result of input of data. (See educe as it is from the same root.)

Educe--To draw out, elicit, lead forth.

Ego--The individual, the self. Ego implies awareness of self and surroundings. A healthy ego is to be distinguished from having an aberrant ego or being on an ego trip, which implies serious limitations in awareness of ones surroundings and their relationship to self. Egocentricity and having an expansive ego are two different directions of ego development. Ego, which is related to or depends upon formative force, is necessary in setting one individual apart from another. Carbon is the carrier for formative force, even as nitrogen is the carrier for astrality and awareness. Plants, though they have egoic force to greater or lesser degree, making them vigorous, are not aware and do not have ego. Animals, insofar as they are unaware of being aware, do not have egoic bodies.

Element--A component part or quality, often one that is basic or essential. Also, in common usage today, any type among 90 or 100 odd atoms with varying positive nuclear charges as detailed in the periodic table of the elements. Kervran (see biological transmutation) discovered transitional types important in the transmutation of elements in the periodic table. In times past element referred to any of the four substances, earth, water, air or fire believed to constitute all matter, but now referred to as the states of matter (solid, liquid, gaseous and radiant (or nascent) states).

Entomology--The study of insects.

Entropy--A measure of the unavailable energy in a thermodynamic system.

Epistemology--The study of how one knows; the theory or science of the method and grounds of knowledge with reference to its limits and validity. For instance, Kant's epistemology set strict limits upon valid acquisition of knowledge, eschewing either intuition or direct cognition.

Ether--The counterpart of matter, having to do with levity, the opposite pole of force to gravity. For any given condition of matter there is permeating it a corresponding ether. Where gravity draws matter toward the center, levity draws the ether toward the outermost extremes. More than any other element, oxygen is the vehicle for etheric influences. The corresponding states of matter and ether from least to greatest intensity are: 1) the radiant (or nascent) state of matter (fire)--and the warmth ether; 2) the gaseous state of matter (air)--and the light ether; 3) the liquid state of matter (water)--and the sound (or chemical) ether; and 4) the solid state of matter (earth)--and the life ether.

Etymology--The origin or derivation of a word. The study of the derivations of words. Often the etymology of a word yields important insights as to its meaning, connotations and the words it is related to.

Euclidean geometry--Proposed by Euclid approximately 300 B.C., euclidean geometry is a point-centered system of defining and relating figures in space where the dimensions are oriented at right angles to each other (orthorotational) and parallel lines are always equidistant (rectilinear). Because it relates forms to the center rather than the periphery, it is well suited for defining physical objects and the effects of gravity and is the geometry commonly taught in our schools. Its pair or dual, counter-euclidean geometry, though still orthorotational and rectilinear, defines and relates figures in space by tangents extending from the surfaces or bounds of forms to the infinite periphery. This geometry is more suited to defining living organisms, the ether, and the effects of levity. One of the features of projective geometry is that geometric systems can be paired in this fashion. (See projective geometry.)

Eurythmy--Harmonious proportion or movement. Also the art or science of word as gesture, the essence of expository dance. The eurythmist, by means of rhythm and harmony of sound and gesture, enacts the essential nature of a symbol, being or thing, thus becoming word/concept, a sparrow, a whale, a tree or the ocean. (See wheat. Also see sympathetic vibratory physics.)

Evil--Cause of limitation, harm, as in an evil or the evil. Also, an adjective used to describe something or someone that causes limitation. From this it may be seen that quite a few things (such as bureaucracies and red tape) are evil that are professed to be "good" or "for your own good."

Evolution--A process of opening out what is contained or implied in something; a transformative process or metamorphosis, as from caterpillar to butterfly or fern to tree. A manifestation of related events or ideas in orderly (not necessarily simple) succession as in a process of development.

Excel--To go beyond or surpass in good qualities or laudable deeds; to outdo or outgo. To exceed or surpass. Virtually all attempts at certifying farm products as quality ones depend on assuring that they meet minimum standards. Probably it is not in the nature of a bureaucracy to ensure excellence, but at least with Demeter certification of a biodynamically grown product the requirements are so stringent they may be interpreted as encouraging the farmer to grow food that is as pure, as balanced, as complete and as full of vitality as possible.

Farm--Originally a parcel of land under lease for cultivation, as the root word means to rent, lease or contract out, as in farming out a job. Now a parcel of land under one management or operated as one unit devoted to agricultural purposes. The etymology of this word implies stewardship rather than ownership.

Fauna--The animals or animal life characteristic of a region or locality, as distinguished from the flora, such as the soil fauna or the fauna of a given field or farm.

Fear of success--One of the most fundamental human fears, also called the non-winner syndrome. This is a phenomenon which plagues people who have a shortage of games. To win or succeed ends the game. Because they would be lost without their game, many people have amazing difficulties any time they come close to success. In prison this is called short timer's disease, as the last six weeks or so before one's release tend to contain an extraordinary number of opportunities to get into further trouble leading to an extended sentence.

Flora--The plants or plant life characteristic of a region or locality.

Fode--To lull into a false sense of security, beguile.

Forb--Any herbaceous plant other than a grass.

Force--The essence of compulsion; that which compels. Modern physics, in a peculiar fit of muddleheadedness, considers there are four forces--the force of gravity, the electromagnetic field force, the strong nuclear interaction, and the weak nuclear interaction. In Goethean, holistic philosophical tradition the forces of nature occur between opposite polarities. Thus there are three forces, 1) the electric force which occurs between positive and negative polarities, 2) the magnetic force which occurs between north and south polarities and 3) the third force of which gravity is one polarity and levity the other. Forces are to be distinguished from fields, which arise from the interaction of two or more forces. The electromagnetic field is one such.

Force of personality--Egoic force. Also vigor. That which empowers a person.

Freedom--The choice to, or not to, or the choice to not choose. As long as one must choose, or one must either have freedom from or freedom for, one is not free but under compulsion. Freedom is relative to perception of choice. Often the most hopelessly enslaved are those who, though they perceive few choices, believe they are free. This is along the same lines as a full vessel cannot receive more, and a know-it-all is unable to learn.

Fringes--The borders or outer edges, also implying looseness, effervescence, insubstantiality or freedom. As used in chapter V, that which is not validated by university research and the conventional scientific community. The most important discoveries tend to be made on the fringes.

Genius--The ability to be, do, have or know one's way, clear of prejudice or convention. One who is free to be, do, have or know apart from the crowd.

Good--Cause of freedom, as in a good person, act, thing or quality or the good ones. Also, an adjective used to describe something or someone who brings about an increase in freedom and ability.

Grass--A monocotyledonous plant, affording feed for cattle, that has narrow, spear-shaped blades with parallel leaf veins, the characteristic leaf gesture where silicon is the predominant element, especially the families Poaceae (true grasses), Cyperaceae (sedges) and Juncaceae (rushes).

Gravity--Ponderability, heaviness, that which imparts the quality of weight.

Hardware cloth--A woven wire mesh, usually made of thin, galvanized or other rust resistant steel wire.

Hectare--A unit of land area equal to 10,000 square meters, 100 ares or 2.471 acres.

Herbaceous--Of or having to do with plants.

Herbivorous--Used to describe an animal that feeds more or less exclusively off olants.

Holistic resource management--A term popularized by Alan Savory, and referring to ways of looking at agriculture and agricultural enterprises in terms of what makes them function as a whole or as wholes within the larger contexts of districts, regions or the world. This acknowledges that a farm cannot be viewed simply in terms of certain crops and their inputs and yields. A farm includes its soils, terrain, geology, weather cycles, the community of plants and animals, the farm family, extended family or support community, the skills, resources, obligations and desires of the people involved, and the cropping and marketing picture as a whole.

Homeopathic dilution--A process of serially diluting and potentizing a remedy. Dilutions commonly are one part in ten, though they can be one in three, one in fifty, one in a hundred, etc. Solid dilutions are usually made with powdered milk sugar and liquid dilutions usually are made with water or in some cases with water with a small percentage of grain alcohol added as a stabilizer. In the case of solid dilutions, potentization is by intensive grinding or mixing (trituration). Liquid dilutions usually are potentized by intensive stirring (dynamization) or shaking (succussion). At each step in the dilution process the remedy is potentized before going on to the next step.

Homeopathic potency--Any specific dilution step of a series made from a remedy, usually designated by both a number and a letter. See Chapter IX.

Homeopathy--The art of curing based on resemblances; the theory and its practice that disease is cured by remedies which produce, with a healthy person, effects similar to the complaint of the patient. The remedies usually are administered in minute doses called homeopathic potencies. Lily Kolisko's research into homeopathic potencies showed that some potencies reinforced the effects of a remedy while other potencies counteracted the remedy's effects. This meant that remedies producing beneficial effects on healthy organisms could be used at some potency to reinforce these beneficial effects. By the same token remedies that produced harmful effects in healthy organisms could be used at other potencies to counteract similar harmful conditions in those who were ill. There are two ideas behind this. One is that any vibratory pattern will be reinforced if the same pattern is added in phase. If that pattern is added out of phase it will be cancelled. Dilution and potentization affect both phase and intensity of vibration. The other idea is that a microscopic change at a point can effect large scale changes in the medium. (See butterfly effect.)

Humus--Complex organic compounds amounting to chaotic or undifferentiated protoplasm from the breakdown of exhausted organic forms.

Humusy--Humus-like or containing an abundance of humus.

Imprimatur--A license to print or publish. Where censorship exists, the stamp of approval on what is published. For example, fringe science, or free science, does not carry the imprimatur of academia and thus, by a process called peer review, is censored out of academically oriented publications.

Infusion--A tea, commonly made by steeping herbs in hot water; also sometimes made by steeping herbs in water in sunlight at ambient temperature (a sun tea).

Integrity--The quality of being whole, unimpaired. A farming operation based on a holistic philosophy of agriculture, for instance, by its very nature has integrity. Farming lacks integrity when it considers nature, with its diversity of species, as an opponent to be conquered by force.

Integrate--To include. To make or become whole, complete. To bring together into a whole. For example, the more species that are integrated into an ecology, the greater the integrity of that ecology.

Koch's postulates--A statement formulated by Robert Koch, a German bacteriologist, in 1881 concerning the conditions permitting microorganisms to cause disease. As follows: 1) The germ must always be found with the disease. 2) It must be isolated in pure culture from the diseased individual. 3) Inoculation with the isolated germs must produce the same disease in a test individual. 4) The germ must be recovered in pure culture from the test individual. At one time known as Koch's laws, these conditions were taken to be invariable. More recently it has been accepted that immunological reactions may replace certain of Koch's postulates. R. R. Rife's work with the first monochromatic microscopes, and Dinshah P. Ghadiali's work with color therapy further confounded Koch's postulates. See postulate.

Kudzu--An extremely vigorous leguminous vine of the arrowroot family, prized in Japan for producing a starchy extract (kuzu). It was spread throughout the southeastern U.S. as a cure for soil erosion in the 1930s. Commonly over 20% protein, it outgrows and smothers any competing vegetation including large trees, but is never seen out of control in well-grazed pastures, as grazing animals eat it to death if given a chance.

Law--A rule, established by authority. Frequently a codified rule of conduct. Laws, such as the laws of physics, the law of diminishing returns, and the state lottery laws are all devised and agreed upon by people, would not exist without people, are held or disavowed and have power only insofar as we engender it. Political laws agreed upon to maintain a polite society sometimes require enforcement, as there are inevitable differences in agreement. A curious fact about such laws is when they are needed most they do the least good. When there are more and more laws and more and more enforcement there is simultaneously a more lawful and a more lawless society. When people exercise common sense and decency there is not much need for laws to govern humans, since humans govern themselves.

Learn--To acquire information or intelligence about; to find out about; to ascertain; to hear. Also to grasp or understand as compared to memorization without comprehension.

Legume--Any of a large group of dicotyledonous plants, variously referred to as an order or family, most of which are characterized by seed pods which split open into two halves with the seeds attached along the inside curvature of the pod. Also well-known for having a symbiotic relationship with nitrogen fixing microorganisms of the genus *Rhizobia*, which live in nodules on the roots of these plants. Legumes exhibit the rounded leaves with branching leaf veins characteristic of calcium. They act as the lungs of the farm organism, drawing nitrogen into association with lime in the soil.

Leonardite--A high humus, sedimentary mineral deposit, somewhat more crumbly than soft coal. It occurs in various localities where ancient sedimentation occurred. Quality for agricultural purposes may vary widely.

Levity--The counterpart of gravity. The quality or state of being light, buoyant.

Life force--Etheric force, force of levity. Foods grown on oxygen deprived soils or without sufficient contact with the clay/humus colloids in the soil tend to be weak in life force. This probably is true for most chemical agriculture crops.

Light--The essential condition of vision, the opposite of darkness. Also, having little weight, insubstantial.

Lime--Used to refer to powdered minerals containing a high proportion of calcium, calcium and magnesium, and various traces of other minerals, usually in the form of carbonates which raise soil pH. When calcium, magnesium and other related elements are added as sulfates, such as gypsum ($CaSO_4$) or epsom salts ($MgSO_4$), these do not raise pH and have a tendency to pass downward into the soil more readily than carbonates.

Machine--In the wider mechanical sense, a more or less complex combination of parts designed to operate in a preconceived and definite manner. This implies automatic operation, without attention or feeling, and has potential for being inappropriate. Stimulus/response behavior amounts to mental machinery, a substitute for knowing exercise of choice in present time. For example, making up one's mind that the next time 'x' happens I will respond in fashion 'y', sets up a mental machine intended to operate without thought, and sooner or later this response will be inappropriate. Generally the more consciously one operates a machine, the more likely one is to avoid its pitfalls.

Mechanical--Of, pertaining to or concerned with machinery. Done as if by machine; uninfluenced by will or emotion; proceeding automatically.

Microorganisms--Any microscopic or ultramicroscopic animal or vegetable organism including protozoans, bacteria, fungi and viruses. Pathogenic (as compared to favorable) microorganisms are those which cause or favor disease.

Minutia--The smallest details. Small or unimportant details.

Money--A medium of exchange or measure of value. We should consider that present forms of money are (1) paper, (2) debased coinage, or in other words coins not worth even close to their face value in metal content, and (3) bookkeeping entries. Certainly money is not to be confused with wealth. (See wealth.)

Moon's nodes--The points where the orbit of the moon intersects the ecliptic. Since the Moon's orbit is inclined at an angle to the plane of the ecliptic, these are two. As the moon goes north, the point where it crosses the ecliptic is called the north node. As it travels back south the point where it crosses the ecliptic is called the south node.

The Moon's nodes (as well as the vernal and autumnal equinoxes) precess (move backward) around the zodiac.

Motility--The capacity to initiate spontaneous movement.

Mycorrhizae--Symbiotic fungi that colonize plant roots, taking sugars and exchanging minerals. In well-aerated, fertile, humusy soils they can increase the mineral uptake of a plant by as much as a factor of ten over the root hairs which they replace. Ants are noted for their ability to establish and culture mycorrhizae.

NPK--An abbreviation commonly used to describe the soluble nitrogen (N), phosphorus (P), and potassium (K) content of fertilizers. For the most part this is a chemical agriculture term used to denote crude soluble salts, saying nothing whatever about colloidal chemistry or life forces.

Occult--Hidden, occluded. To be distinguished from mystical, magical or imaginary. Something that is largely hidden or occult in the world today is the working of the third force. (See force, radionics.)

Occultation--An occurrence where one heavenly body (usually the Sun or Moon) obscures another, as in "The Moon occults Venus at 2:43 p.m. on Thursday."

Ontology--The science of being. The study of all that is, both physical and non-physical. Ontology is basic to holistic thinking.

Organic--Pertaining to or derived from living organisms, exhibiting characteristics peculiar to living organisms. To be distinguished from pertaining to that branch of chemistry dealing with synthetic carbon compounds and called organic chemistry.

Organic farming--Variously defined by certification and regulatory agencies, this refers in general to any agricultural method that eschews the use of chemical fertilizers and toxic chemicals. The idea of organic farming was popularized by J. I. Rodale as part of his concern for nutrition. While organic farming masquerades as materialism, it recognizes that food need not only be non-toxic, it must contain vital nourishment. Salt fertilizers rarely produce foods with the vitality of those grown with compost, sand, ashes, humus, rock powder, tilth, timely planting, sufficient rain and a little care and attention. Much illness results from weakness of the etheric body. Organic growing generally produces foods of greater vitality, which is why organically grown foods are often recommended by wellness counselors and alternative health care professionals.

Orgone energy--A term coined by Wilhelm Reich referring to life force or the ether. He distinguished healthy orgone energy from what he termed *oranur*, an overexcited or feverish condition of the ether. Even further, there was a stagnant, toxic or necrotic condition of the ether which he termed *DOR*, or deadly orgone energy. The implications of this for agriculture are even today only dimly perceived.

Orgonomy--The study of orgone energy as established by Wilhelm Reich. Reich blazed trails investigating life energy, how to detect it and measure it, collect it, modify it and utilize it. He found that one could accumulate orgone energy in a metallic container that had a covering of organic material. These containers could be intensified by alternate layering of metallic and organic materials, as long as the outermost layer was organic and the innermost was metallic. Certain types and combinations of metallics (such as galvanized steel) and organics (such as rabbit fur) are better collectors of either OR or DOR. In effect the Earth itself is an accumulator. As we have stripped the forests and prairie bare and depleted the topsoils of humus, we have left metallic subsoils exposed, thus reversing the Earth's accumulation of orgone energy. The Earth's magnetic field has declined as its vitality has diminished. This helps explain why moldboard plowing, which buries crop residues, forces soils into decline, and why chisel plowing, where crop residues remain on or near the surface, tends to have a soil building effect. This also explains why spreading rock powder without having a mulch of some sort covering it can have a downturn effect on soil vitality.

Paramagnetic--Having a greater magnetization than a vacuum. Having a magnetic permeability of more than unity. Magnetic. A paramagnetic material is attracted (to the magnet) in the vicinity of a magnet. To be distinguished from diamagnetic. (See diamagnetic.)

Periphery--The outer bounds of a thing as distinguished from its internal regions or center.

Permaculture--A term popularized by Bill Mollison, referring to a diverse compendium of methods whereby one grows food within the context of more or less permanently established communities of plants and animals, enhancing rather than diminishing or deranging these communities. This takes advantage of synergy, the positive effect of cooperation between different species, and usually avoids such things as weeding or cultivation.

pH--A chemical symbol denoting the negative logarithm of the concentration of hydrogen ions in gram atoms per liter. In layman's terms this is a measure of acidity or alkalinity where a pH of 7 is neutral (as acid as it is alkaline), 6 is ten times as acid, 5 is a hundred times as acid, 4 a thousand times, etc. Likewise a pH of 8 is ten times as alkaline as neutral, 9 is a hundred times, 10 a thousand times, etc.

Planetary nodes--With any given planet, the points where, either going north or south, the planet's orbit intersects the ecliptic.

Plant--An organism lacking in locomotor or any rapid motor response and having no nervous or sensory organs. A vegetable in the broad sense, as distinguished from an animal. Also something planned to a "T" and established, as with a sewage treatment plant, or once again, a vegetable.

Polled--Without horns. Usually this refers to a breed of cattle (polled cattle) such as Angus or Herefords that do not develop horns. In politics, having to do with counting heads, as in "They polled the farm vote."

Postulate--A statement taken as true without proof. A postulate may not be provable, or later may prove wrong. Also to demand, require, claim or stipulate. To claim as true, real or existent.

Potentization--In homeopathy the process of dynamizing, (stirring) succussing (shaking) or triturating (grinding) a remedy.

Precambrian--Relating to the earliest geologic age, presently believed to date from 600 million years ago backwards. Actually geology is wrong in many of its assumptions. What is done to estimate the character and duration of past geological ages is comparable to examining a calf at six weeks old, doing so again at six months and six years, and using these data to extrapolate how this calf appeared 600 and 60,000 years ago. Such extrapolations do not apply and lead to erroneous conclusions. The Earth is not merely aging, but is evolving, as from caterpillar to butterfly.

Projective geometry--A study of all geometric systems. That branch of geometry that deals with spatial relations, ideas and properties unaltered by transformations of space, which send points into points, lines into lines, planes into planes, and any two incident elements into two incident elements. One of the features of projective geometry is that geometric systems are paired, as, for example, the euclidean and counter-euclidean geometries are an orthorotational (dimensions are oriented at right angles to one another) and rectilinear (parallel lines are always equidistant and the shortest distance between two points is a straight line) dual. (See euclidean geometry.) Other non-euclidean geometric duals are known for which the assumptions of orthorotation and rectiliniarity do not hold.

PTO--In farming parlance, a power take off unit, usually part of a tractor or truck transmission.

Radionics--The study of a kind of force that works directly upon the nuclei of atoms; not recognized by most modern physicists. Regardless of the current belief amongst physicists that there are four forces (i.e. electromagnetic, gravitational and the strong and weak nuclear interactions), there are but three forces, the force of magnetism, the force of electricity and the third force or nuclear force which works directly with matter and is not fully discovered yet. (See force.) Between these three forces there may be four kinds of interactions--electromagnetic, electronuclear, magnetonuclear and electromagnetonuclear. The so-called radionic manifestations of the nuclear force are not bound by the inverse square law (meaning radionic energy does not diminish as the square of the distance from its source increases), nor are they limited to the speed of light. Discovery of radionics is credited to Dr. Albert Abrams, who in the 1920s made his observations in the course of his medical practice and built the first radionic devices. At first he believed he had discovered some property of electricity, but later found the rules for electrical phenomena did not all apply. Radionic devices allow the operator to effect changes in the vibratory patterns of subjects. They are notable for the ease with which they alter plants and animals, but radionic devices may fail to work on human beings when their egoic bodies interfere. As with dowsing, moral and spiritual development increases the effectiveness of the operator. (See also dowse, sympathetic vibratory physics.)

Radionic device--Any device or instrument making use of radionic energy. T. Galen Hieronymus performed extensive studies of what materials served to conduct or insulate from this energy and how it might be be modified, amplified and applied. Hieronymus received the only U.S. patent ever awarded a radionic device. Radionic devices come in three basic types, variable capacitance, variable inductance and variable impedance. Since radionic devices are outlawed for medical practice in the U.S. (though they are widely used in England), they find their commonest application in agriculture, where many minor miracles have been wrought with them. Research money is hard to come by in this field as it threatens to upset the big applecarts.

Reality--The state, character, quality, or fact of being real, existent, self-existent or genuine, or of having real being or existence.

Religion--The service or adoration of God or a god. Also a system of faith, worship or belief. The term derives from the Latin, *religio*, *religare*, which refer to binding or holding back. Insofar as it is the profession of faith, worship or belief in what one is told or supposed to believe, religion tends to be limiting and to lead to spiritual stagnation or degeneration. When religion involves developing one's beliefs and living one's life by them (or giving up one's life for them) it tends to lead to greater freedom and ability, and spiritual growth. Yet, what serves to inspire one person may seem to another to be stultifying and confining, as religions must reconcile absolute values with the ways these values are received and responded to from individual viewpoints. (See belief, good, evil, educate.)

Rhizobia--Any of a genus of very small, rod-shaped bacteria of the family *Nitrobacteriacea*, living symbiotically in nodules produced on the roots of leguminous plants, where they fix atmospheric nitrogen. In general they are species specific for the legume they interact with. That is, soybeans, alfalfa, birdsfoot trefoil and peanuts all require different species of *Rhizobia* for effective nodulation. *Rhizobia* nodulate well only when soil nitrogen is depleted, thus they do the most good following root or grain crops, such as carrots and turnips or corn and wheat that either do not receive compost, or which use up most of the available nitrogen.

Science--Knowledge possessed as a result of study and practice. Also, any branch or department of systematized knowledge considered as a distinct field of investigation, as physics or the life sciences. (See Chapter VII.) Also (vulgar) a modern belief system that assumes objective pursuit of truth, experimentation, questioning of authority, and yet is mired in the most wildly implausible of all philosophies, materialism. It is not the posing of questions or the experimentation that is so bad about this kind of science, but its theorizing, as this is founded on postulates which necessitate rejecting all but the data of the senses, and even some of that. This is called one-eyed, color blind science. Insofar as the layman generally takes science on faith, adoring or worshiping the scions of science and their explanation of what is, science is his religion.

Sense--Sensuous perception, now especially used to describe aesthetic or emotional perception. Also, one of the avenues of perception, as in the so-called five senses. As a verb, to have consciousness of, feel, perceive. Also to perceive by the senses.

Sidereal--Of or relating to the stars or constellations. Measured by the apparent motion of fixed stars. Designated, marked out or accompanied by a return to the same position in respect to the stars, as in a sidereal day, sidereal year or sidereal time. The difference between standard (solar) time and sidereal time is that standard time is measured by the Sun's return to the meridian, whereas sidereal time is measured by the return of a designated star (usually Regulus) to the meridian. Solar and sidereal time are not the same due to the Earth's travel in its orbit around the Sun. A sidereal day is roughly 3 minutes and 56 seconds shorter than the average solar day. Accordingly, there is one more sidereal day per year than there are solar days.

Sidereal astrology--A study of the motions of the bodies of the solar system against the background of the actual constellations rather than the signs of the tropical zodiac. (See astrology.)

Silicic acid--Any of various weakly acidic substances obtained as gelatinous masses by treating certain silicates with acids. Also occurring in other ways, such as occurring naturally in living organisms, composts and glacial melt waters. Silicic acids are not obtained in pure form, and are held by some not to be true compounds. They may be classed according to the number of silicon atoms in the molecule, such as monosilicic acids (H_4SiO_4 and H_2SiO_5) or polysilicic acids ($H_2Si_2O_5$, $H_4Si_3O_8$, etc.). Silicic acid is important in living organisms as a carrier of cosmic forces.

Soil--The upper layer or layers of earth which may be dug, plowed, excavated, etc.; specifically the loose surface material of the earth in which plants grow.

Space--That which is characterized by extension in all directions, boundlessness and indefinite divisibility; that in which all physical things are ordered and related at one time (or apart from time); the subject of determinations of position and direction.

Spiritual--Of or pertaining to or consisting of spirit; not material; incorporeal.

String theorists--Physicists attempting to work out a unified field theory (i.e. one theory to explain and predict all phenomena) based on the idea that the basic units of matter are not particles in the sense of little balls, but rather are tiny needles or strings, subject to being aligned, non-aligned or mis-aligned.

Subtle energies--Also called low level energies or vibrations. These are not strong energies in the sense of what drives machines like automobiles or newspaper presses. Rather they are subtle rhythms and harmonies of vibration--complex patterns of coherent energy such as may be found in music or in the long (infrared) or extra long (ELF) wavelengths. Many things generate or modify subtle energies. (See also: orgone, radionics, sympathetic vibratory physics.)

Succussion--Act of shaking; the fact or state of being shaken, especially with violence.

Sustainable agriculture--A term applied to methods of farming which avoid many of the worst abuses of chemical agriculture. This is a step in the right direction regardless of thinking in terms of hanging in there with maybe just a little shortfall. It may provide fertile ground for planting the seeds of enthusiastically regenerative methods which restore diversity, thrift, symbiosis and synergy, and point the way out of shortage into abundance.

Symbiosis--The living together in intimate, cooperative association of two or more dissimilar organisms or types of organisms, usually resulting in benefit to each. (See mycorrhizae, *Rhizobia*.)

Sympathetic magic--A production of seemingly miraculous results by use of likenesses and mimicry to enlist the aid of hidden forces in nature. This is only magic insofar as the way it works is a mystery to most observers. (See below.)

Sympathetic vibratory physics--A term coined in the 19th century by John E. W. Keely to describe his investigations into the nature of the universe. He found that all things are related, as they are all composed of vibrations. Force is liberated matter and matter is force in bondage. All materials and conditions result from variations in basic vibrations and their harmonics, according to amplitude, velocity, mode, sympathy, number and periodicity. He developed devices which could be turned on or off simply by the operator having thoughts which were in sympathy with the operation of the device, and he accomplished tasks ranging from levitation of massive objects to healing mental illnesses with sound. To varying degrees his devices employed forces that so far have been relegated to the scientific fringes. Steiner forecast that a time would come when much of what is accomplished today by physical labor in agriculture and day-to-day living would be accomplished simply by thought, making use of the laws of sympathetic vibrations. As he put it, "The famous technology of our days will come to its end soon because she will in a certain way wind up herself. The following phenomenon will then appear; man will achieve the faculty to employ the fine vibrations of his ethereal body to impulsate mechanical devices. The individual will be able to transmit his own vibrations to the machine, and only he will be able to set the machine in motion by the vibrations generated by himself. The men who are now practical technicians will soon discover they are standing before a complete change as to what one calls practical, when man will be involved with his *will* in the objective *feeling* of the world." It has been said that sympathetic vibratory physics is as important to mankind's spiritual and moral growth as it is to his material benefit. Like dowsing and radionics this science cannot be fully mastered without having first mastered self, and this implies eliminating sub-conscious counter-intentions and conflicts and becoming aware of being connected to everything in one's surroundings.

Synergy--The working together of various organisms and/or agencies whereby the overall effect is greater than if they worked separately. For example, two pastures, one planted in grasses and one in legumes, will not produce as much in sum as if they both were planted in a mixture of grasses and legumes. Synergy is a feature of life and diversity, and exemplifies the idea that the community of different species taken as a whole is greater than the sum of its parts taken individually. Where the community of different species is sufficiently diverse and harmonious the synergistic effect can be strongly regenerative. (See also symbiosis.)

Threefold social order--A social concept based on the threefoldness of man. In the social realm human society is made up of the significance sphere (this includes art, science, philosophy and religion), the political sphere, in which people work toward agreement and cooperation, and the economic sphere, which deals with the production of our daily bread and other such valuable items of exchange. These parallel the physical human being with his head, heart and guts, and the spiritual human with his thought, emotion and will. Presently in western society, particularly in the U.S., certain elements within the economic sphere predominate, so that economic forces drive the arts, sciences and religion, as well as the political processes. Until these spheres come into balance and we establish each domain as free from domination by the others, we will have social turmoil. This same principle of balance and stability lies at the basis of individual physical and spiritual health. Just as the heart mediates between the head and the guts, and the emotions mediate between thinking and volition, the political sphere must mediate between the significance realm of our ideals and the economic realm of everyday necessity. Democratic institutions, insofar as they have not risen above being a dictatorship of a majority and conducting a popularity contest between stooges representing competing special interest factions, have not accomplished much along these lines. Insofar as individuals in the political sphere have attempted to fulfill their roles as mediators, the trend in political initiatives has been toward reaching consensus. Where political efforts have been partisan either to ideals or personal economic gains, this has involved the unwilling sacrifice of liberty on the part of some of the people involved.

Third force--A term used by Steiner to describe nuclear force, or a force beyond electricity and magnetism, under investigation on the scientific fringes. (See Chapter II. Also see force.)

Tithe--A tenth part. Experientially something you may hear about in a sermon before the collection plate is passed. Originally intended as a reinvestment of a tenth part of one's income into the well-being of society. If a business enterprise reinvests a tenth of its proceeds in improvement of its business it will surely prosper. Likewise if we reinvest a tenth part of our personal incomes in such unselfish endeavors as education, spiritual discovery, care of the environment and help for misfits and unfits, our whole society will prosper. However, this cannot be done carelessly. For instance, if we give our tithe to the public schools and they accomplish little in terms of education, we might as well be flushing our tenth part down a sewer.

Toxic--That which has a poisonous or ill effect. The cause of harmful effects, thought of as an unnatural, often slow, cause of death.

Transfinite--Beyond or surpassing any finite number, having to do with the fact there are both definite and infinite infinities.

Transformative--Having power to change in structure or composition.

Trituration--A process of rubbing, grinding, bruising or thrashing. The process of rubbing or grinding to a very fine or impalpable powder thorough pulverization. Trituration, usually with a mortar and pestle, is used to potentize homeopathic preparations in solid form (usually diluted in milk sugar).

Truth--Fidelity, constancy. Conformity to fact or reality; the property of being in accord with what is, has been or must be.

Vitality--The state or quality of being lively; the principle of life.

Void--Containing nothing, empty, vacant. That which is empty or unfilled space.

Vortex--A mass of fluid having a whirling motion and tending to form a cavity or vacuum in the center of its axis, as a whirlpool is a vortex. Also a collection of subtle force lines endowed with rapid rotatory motion around an axis such as that of a planet or sun. Descartes devised a vortex theory to account for the formation of the universe. Accordingly there may be either in or out vortices, explaining how the universe appears to be expanding on the grand scale even while in various localities collapse is seen to occur.

Vortexya--Universal force. Vortex force.

Warmth--Quality or state of being warm in temperature; also in feeling or emotional intensity.

Wealth--Well being, abundant possession of things which are objects of human desire. A measure to which one possesses things of value or the means of obtaining them. Riches. Not to be confused with money, although money may be a means of obtaining certain things of value.

Wheat--Along with rice and corn, one of the most important agricultural plants. Believed to have originated in central Asia, it is any annual grass of the species *Triticum*, especially *Triticum vulgare*, which grows vigorously in cold weather and ripens nutritious grains (called wheat berries) in the heat of summer. The English word wheat derives from the idea of eat. But, unlike meat, which is a thoroughly grounded form of eat, this is upright, as in heat, and it aims for the zenith at the same time as it connects across the board (H). Even more, as it reaches to the heavens for energy it opens itself to spiritual forces from the wide expanses (W). Thus wheat reveals its significance, not only by its gesture as a plant, but also by the gestures of its letters. Much of the significance of a language is of this nature, although this frequently is not recognized. Eurythmy sometimes is used as a tool to elucidate the meanings of words. (See eurythmy.)

Will--Power coupled with desire or intention; the act or experience of willing; volition. Also disposition toward activity, as for example, only his will kept him going. The will of the spiritual human being works in conjunction with his metabolic functions or his guts.

Wisdom--Ability to judge soundly and deal sagaciously with facts, especially as they relate to life and conduct. Knowledge along with the capacity to make use of it. Perception of the best ends and the best means.

Words--Articulate sounds or series of sounds which, through association with fixed meanings, symbolize and communicate ideas. Also written or printed characters or collections of characters symbolizing spoken words. (See above, wheat.)

Zodiac--The belt of constellations surrounding the plane of the ecliptic; also called the animal circle. These constellations are twelve, named, in order of clockwise travel, Aries, the ram; Taurus, the bull; Gemini, the twins; Cancer, the crab; Leo, the lion; Virgo, the virgin; Libra, the balance or scales; Scorpio, the scorpion or eagle; Sagittarius, the archer; Capricorn, the goat; Aquarius, the waterbearer; and Pisces, the fishes.

Chapter I

From early on I wanted to understand life. I studied business, sociology, biochemistry and religion toward that end, but found these all fell short of my mark.

A time came when I realized that helping others was an integral part of helping myself. And, in becoming a psychologist I believe I helped a few people. Certainly I helped myself. On the whole, however, it seemed to me my efforts yielded too little result.

People would come to realizations in therapy and then forget them and fail to apply them. Clients kept coming back with the same sorts of problems, and I knew I was not getting to the causes. The thought kept growing in my mind that, more than anything, people had insufficient force of personality to stabilize their gains. They had insufficient power of will to turn thinking into action.

Why? Gradually it occurred to me that even the best therapies, like ministries, were putting the cart before the horse. The most fundamental, everyday things deserved the greatest emphasis, and I believed that nutrition and environment were amongst the most basic things. My clients and I were trying to live on devitalized and contaminated food, water, air and sunshine. How could we hope for physical, let alone mental and spiritual well-being?

This led me to try to farm. I wanted to grow quality food that nourished the will and imparted force of personality. But, as a city boy I had little experience with farming. My first year I raised sorghum for syrup because it did not require much chemical fertilizer and no pesticides. Yet, this cost me heavily.

By year's end all I had accomplished was selling off fertility for sub-minimum wages. Farming this way I would go bankrupt. I began to see that farmers everywhere were doing this, and it made no sense. No wonder they were treated like chumps and given the short end of the stick by other professionals. They sold off their capital, called it net income, and paid taxes on it. I made up my mind to invest whatever I could into soil fertility, especially since I could write it off as an expense. I imagined an organic approach would build soil.

I was told that organic farming was not feasible, or that if it could be done it might take ten years to convert. Moreover, on the large scale there were not enough organic fertilizers, especially manures, for all farmers to farm organically anyway.

While I figured this was propaganda I still did not know how to proceed. In the end what it took was a new way of thinking.

"When you learn to love hell, you will be in heaven."

– Thaddeus Golas

A New Way of Thinking

Some of my earliest farming errors lay in my failure to understand humus.

I borrowed a neighbor's moldboard (turning) plow and dealt death to the blackberries, the sod and all the little clumps of brush. It gave me a clean seedbed, burying my topsoil and organic residues deep. I thought they would surely not wash away, and that such plowing would make my soil rich.

I just assumed that the organic matter I plowed under would become rich humus down there.

I could plow deeper when the soil was moist, so I preferred to plow three days after a soaking rain. On my heavy clay soils that meant creating plowpan, but I did not know. What was plowpan?

I disced the soil too wet also. This made an abundance of rock-like clods roughly the size of baseballs as well as packing the clay deeper down. Everything I plowed under was closed off from the air, and it putrefied, leaching into the water table instead of being converted to humus. But, I did not know.

More Early Errors

My first year I grew sorghum cane and hauled it to a local syrup mill. I used 6-12-12 fertilizer and returned nothing to the field. But now I really had problems. The soil had a terrible tendency to crust when it rained. Heavy rains were causing erosion and quagmires. Soil tests showed only one and a half percent organic matter. I figured I could correct that simply enough, and I hauled all the sawdust and fresh manure I could get to my fields.

I plowed it under deep. Around my raspberries and asparagus, and wherever I could not plow, I mulched six inches deep with manure and sawdust. I figured the more organic matter the better.

But something was wrong. The rhubarb, which was a robust clump near the old kitchen compost pile, died from this treatment. I began to suspect that compost was good, so I tried making a pile. But I had no idea about balancing air, moisture and soil. I dug a pit and filled it with wet dairy manure mixed with spoiled corn silage. I covered this with a truckload of fresh sawdust and really did expect the best results. However, it sat there pickled and anaerobic instead of composting.

Meanwhile I found a local sawmill that burned their slabs and had a vast reserve of wood ashes. I hauled load after load, spreading it on thick, thinking here was a rich mineral source. It surelyq was. In one spot the pH went up to 8.3, and nothing would grow.

Additionally, I thought I did not need animals. What a lot of bother. Besides, manure was being wasted on nearby farms, and both sawmills and sorghum mills had plenty of residues. Why feed my stuff to animals when they would just chew it up and extract valuable nutrients? I thought it best to turn everything under as deep as possible to make the soil rich.

Having a balanced and diverse ecology was just an abstraction to me. All I really knew were my preconceived ideas.

Meeting Peter Escher

In my second year I was fortunate to meet a frail and wizened old fellow named Peter Escher. He was startlingly perceptive and blunt. In twenty minutes I realized he knew more about nature and agriculture than I had thought possible.

Within seconds of arriving at my upper field he started telling me the errors I had been making.

"Too much raw manure. You should compost everything. How deep have you been plowing? Dig a hole and let's see. You've plowed this too wet."

"But," I protested, "I always wait three days after a rain."

"Nevertheless, you've plowed it too wet. See?" He pointed out my abundance of rock-like lumps of hard clay.

"What is this with your fruit trees?"

Peter started clawing away at the deep mulch of shavings and small stones around the trees. He showed no sign of letting up, so I helped him. By the time I had a radius of a foot cleared around the trunks of a couple trees he was showing me signs of borers which were causing severe damage. But, he refused to blame the borers themselves. Instead he said I was using too much raw manure.

He pointed out fire blight and told me again, "Too much raw manure."

"I only put on a little. I didn't have enough to put on a lot," I told him.

"Was it chicken manure?" he asked.

"Yes."

"Anyway, it was too much."

He wandered on with me in tow, spellbound by his easy insights into my activities. He pointed out the weak stalks of my winter grains, showing me where they were planted too thickly and where the raw manure had been applied. He pointed out spots on the stems that I had not noticed.

"What's that?" I asked.

"Whatever it is, it doesn't belong there."

Again and again he showed me disease and insect problems that came from incorporation of uncomposted manures and organic residues.

Biodynamic Agriculture

"Use the preps and compost everything," Peter advised. "And, you need stinging nettle."

Stinging nettle, I later found, is an herb used by biodynamic farmers to promote better circulation. From upstate New York, he mailed me a start of this herb.

I began using Dr. Pfeiffer's Field Spray and Dr. Pfeiffer's Quick Composting Compound, which incorporate the biodynamic preparations (BD preps.) He also gave me the address of Josephine Porter, who made and sold all the various BD preps.

I still plowed badly, but at least I was not turning under such massive quantities of organic matter to putrefy in anaerobic rottenness. I slacked off on my heavy mulches and some of the fungi decreased. I saved part of the asparagus patch by peeling the mulch back. I lost some apple trees to borers and a cherry and a plum tree to fungus, but the rest improved.

For my last, heavy, raw manure application I used fifty tons of fresh cow manure on half of a three acre field. On the other half I used a few ounces of Dr. Pfeiffer's Field Spray. I expected more out of the manured half. Quite honestly, I had trouble accepting Peter's advice despite his confidence, insight and authority. Surely plowing under fifty tons of cow manure would have far more fertilizer value than plowing under a few ounces of Dr. Pfeiffer's Field Spray. But, the soil in the half treated with the biodynamic treatment became dark and crumbly, while the half that was cow manured remained a light colored, sodden clay where crusting and weeds were a problem.

Compost and Topsoil

On a return visit, Peter examined my compost piles, pointing out that the layers were far too thick. They should never be much over an inch deep for any one layer. He rubbed some of the compost around on his palm for a couple of minutes, just feeling it and looking at it. Then he smelled it and, to my immense surprise, he tasted it! He appeared only marginally satisfied. He cautioned me to use more soil in my piles and to keep on using the preps. He emphasized calling earth "soil" and not "dirt," the nuances of which escaped me at the time.

He was especially excited about the morphology of my fall radish plantings, which I thought were a flop. They were from home saved seed, and instead of big roots they had swollen stems rather similar to kohlrabi. He ate a couple right there in the garden, and indicated I had bred a new variety of vegetable. But, the winter freezes killed them and I had no other seed.

Several of my grandiose plans for landscaping he punctured like the bubble-headed pipe dreams that they were. In general his rule was to move as little soil as possible.

On a third visit he finally made some impression on me about not inverting the soil with turning plows. He spotted a place where I had dumped a wheelbarrow load of obvious subsoil in a low spot. He showed me numerous signs of trouble related to this one wheelbarrow load of lifeless subsoil smothering the richer, air-loving humus of my topsoil.

"Always leave your topsoil on top," he emphasized, finally getting this important message through.

Remembering Peter Escher

Peter died in May of 1984, but I remember him as one of the most influential figures in my overcoming the wrong-headed ideas I had. And although the biodynamic preparations were somewhat incomprehensible at first, the clear and extraordinary authority Peter expressed in both words and body language served to convince me to try them.

I realized biodynamic farmers knew something I needed to learn when the few ounces of Dr. Pfeiffer's Field Spray, stirred and sprayed in the afternoon just before plowing, resulted in much greater soil improvement than fifty tons of cow manure at roughly forty times the cost in both cash and labor.

I found biodynamics was a philosophy of agriculture that viewed the biosphere as a living organism made up of varying combinations of earth, water, air and fire between the cosmic (silica) pole and the earthly (lime) pole of nature.

Since then I have been through a lot. But Peter stands alone as someone who put his hands right on and right into my experience and was unhesitatingly outspoken about what he found. Though he was clearly of the most fragile health and advanced age, his energetic outlook on life astonished me.

Two things I will never forget about him. One was his enthusiastic reverence, which perhaps was most apparent in his repeated advice to me to pray and to plant more flowers. The other was his response to a question about his age. He chuckled, seeming to sparkle, and said, "I'm at least twice as old as you think I am."

Chapter II

What makes biodynamic agriculture so different from other methodologies? When I first became acquainted with biodynamic agriculture, I wrote to Heinz Grotzke, then editor of the Biodynamic Association's quarterly, Biodynamics. I confided that I was uncomfortable with the term "biodynamic." I disliked the thought that chemical growers were calling their toxic methods "agriculture" while more responsible growers used extra terms like they were part of some fringe group. It was clear to me that biodynamic agriculture was simply good agriculture.

Heinz wrote back that whatever things might someday be like, right now when people thought of agriculture, they thought of chemical methods. Biodynamic agriculture had to distinguish itself from the chemical aberrations to avoid being tarred with the same brush. It even had to be distinguished from organic agriculture, since organic agriculture was bogged down with materialistic thinking.

Heinz went on to explain that bio refers to life and organisms while dynamic refers to the changing, cyclical rhythms of nature. Thus biodynamic agriculture refers to a way of farming that is full of life, rhythm and variety.

Biodynamic agriculture deals in a balanced, integrated way with both the vegetative and the animated. And, it not only recognizes the existence of organic materials, but also the existence of forces which affect these materials in a dynamic fashion.

Heinz made a deep impression, though I maintain it is unfair for chemical agriculture, in all its myopic carelessness, to be perceived as "the" agriculture. But, he was right. We must live with our nomenclature until such times as the tables turn.

What Is Biodynamic Agriculture?

It is the oldest organic agricultural movement in the western world. In the early twentieth century certain German farmers were noticing a loss of vitality in land, crops and seeds. They asked Rudolf Steiner for help, and biodynamic agriculture developed from his agriculture course, a series of eight lectures on the subject.

It is poetic justice that biodynamic agriculture was born in the German world, as it was a German, Justus von Liebig, who is hailed as the father of chemical agriculture. To shed light on this dichotomy it may help to detail how holistic science developed in Europe, and how this differed from analytical viewpoints.

Holistic Science

More than any other in the late 19th and early 20th centuries, Rudolf Steiner advocated holistic science. In this he followed Goethe, who as a poet, playwright and scientist, championed holistic thinking and scientific endeavor when holism had little going for it besides demoralized and inarticulate peasant roots.

In Goethe's time, analytical science was gaining a full head of steam. Could it be fixed in space, measured, weighed, quantified? If not, forget it. Forget the context. Forget the implications. Forget the long-range view. Such was the thinking in Europe, and its raw power was something the world had to acknowledge. In the face of this Goethe was a lone voice crying out.

Significantly, he considered his scientific efforts the most important, and felt his poetry was a by-product. Amongst others of his time he stood alone. What set Goethe apart so?

Color Theory

Color theory was a watershed issue. Newton had theorized that color resulted from the division of white light into different wavelengths. But, Goethe observed some things which Newton ignored.

Newton studied color by shining a light through a slit in an opaque shield, through a prism and onto a screen. He held that only light was involved. Goethe pointed out, however, that color arose with a prism *only* at the boundary between light and darkness. Indeed, Newton's light through a slit was such a boundary. Where Newton theorized that the phenomenon of color could be reduced to the action of a single force, Goethe showed that the experiments actually revealed the interaction of two opposite forces.

In general Goethe strove to fathom the whole, whatever its complexity, while the prevailing scientific fashion was to reduce things to the utmost simplicity. This has earned modern science the sobriquet of reductionism.

The difference between analytical science and holism ran deeper. Could a science that dealt with limited facts in isolation be as *good* as a science that dealt with facts in their overall context? Analytical science dealt only with the physical, and avoided the issue of good entirely. Taken by itself, a thing was neither good nor bad. It simply was. Analytical science examined facts in isolation. It did not face the issue of good.

Goethe, however, perceived that in the material world activity arose out of the principle of polarity, and in the spiritual world the principle of enhancement gave rise to action. Thus he not only saw deeply into physical reality, but he faced even the spiritual issue of what was good.

In this way Goethe stood alone as a proponent of holism, despite being dismissed by the analytical school with mutterings of, "Why doesn't he stick to poetry?"

Goethe's love for combining the artful and the mundane--his realization that the qualitative goes hand in hand with the quantitative--was demonstrated in his treatise, *The Metamorphosis Of Plants*. Instead of looking at plant forms frozen in specimen collections, he looked at plants as dynamic entities expressing rhythm and function, things intangible and ephemeral and yet ever so real. The idea that science could only give credence to the corpse-- ignoring the vital principle--seemed absurd to Goethe. Fortunately, he passed on this viewpoint, as his investigations were a starting point for Steiner.

The Good, the Valuable, the Qualitative

Steiner faced an uphill battle against the entrenched analytical mindset. Even now holism has hardly gotten scientists to ask themselves, "What is the good of science? "

Starting from the work of Goethe, Steiner's studies were extremely broad, as shown by his thousands of lectures and manuscripts. In one area after another he pointed out fundamental principles, giving general indications and encouraging further investigations.

He also gave specific, practical indications, as for example in his agriculture lectures with their instructions for making the agricultural medicines now known as the BD preps.

So, biodynamic agriculture owes its existence to a philosophical tradition separate and contrapuntal to chemical agriculture's. Biodynamics requires a different viewpoint--one that in Goethe's words looks toward the good, the valuable, the qualitative.

The Squeeze

Steiner studied all aspects of human society, not just agriculture, as his lectures on world economy and his *Threefold Social Order* make clear. He was well aware that farmers have lost control over costs as well as the prices they receive. In the marketplace they get nailed.

Dealers in storable commodities can tell buyers to pay cost plus profit or come back later. Farmers, however, deal with perishables. All too often they have to take whatever they can get. This means they get squeezed. Though theirs is the initiative and the risk, they have insufficient leverage.

On biodynamic farms, balance and diversity help avoid these marketplace pressures. If one does not get a high enough price the crop may be fed to the animals and recycled as fertilizer. Only a small percentage of the total biomass production of the farm is ever exported.

By working toward self-sufficiency the biodynamic grower is in a more favorable position. To get his farm going he may invest considerable labor and expertise, but he does not require so much money. Due to the high quality of his products he tends to experience a growing demand. Most BD growers could sell more if they produced it.

Much of the economy of a biodynamic farm depends on using the BD preps. Artfully made and applied, these are medicines for healing the earth. Chemical farming tends to be indifferent to healing the earth, or its proponents may even maintain the earth is not ill. Regardless, it is the nature of humanity to strive toward fuller expression of freedom and ability. Using the BD preps to effect the earth's healing is part and parcel of unfolding the talents and abilities of a free humanity.

Skillful use of the preps can reduce the need for composted manure. In the long run there need be no fertilizer shortage. A farm can generate its own fertility once it is thriving. This alone would set farmers free.

Genesis of the Preps

Steiner introduced the preps from a profound grasp of nature. For example, in making BD 500 (horn manure) he took dung from a cow, a ruminant that focuses its being upon digestion to the extent its dung virtually becomes pudding. This is a creature so introverted and meditative that we think of these qualities when we use the verb *to ruminate*, which means to chew over or ponder.

Steiner packed this dung into a cow horn and buried it in the Earth for the entire winter, even somewhat into the spring--perhaps from October or November until May or June. This made a material that was a model fertility input. A handful stirred energetically in three gallons of water was sufficient to treat an entire acre.

Inevitably questions arise. Why a cow's horn? Why the winter? Why cow manure? Why the stirring and application of such small amounts per acre? To answer these questions let us look at other holistic traditions besides the one of Goethe and Steiner.

In America, for example, the native medicine people were keenly perceptive of the overall connections in nature. They made medicines out of natural materials such as horns, dung, rocks and herbs. Commonly they would use a pinch here, a few drops there, or perhaps a handful at some key point. They could do this with assurance because they saw the true nature of things. Nature wears her signatures in plain sight. The signs are there, but without an appreciation of the cycles, functions, forms, progressions and interrelatedness of events, in short the *values*, these signs go unnoticed.

The Significance of the Cow

Looked at in wide perspective, the animal kingdom's nervous development is supported by digestion, and digestion is supported and enhanced by motility and the choice of what will be eaten. The nervous system, particularly the brain, is an expression of the digestive impulse taken to a higher stage of development. Indeed, the brain looks similar to the intestines.

Clearly, human beings use their nervous systems to express their spiritual potential, their value to the world. But, despite well-developed nervous systems they are not the most digestive creatures. This is the bovine's role. In this we see the ancient reason the cow was sacred in India and why the land where the buffalo roamed has given rise to so much inventiveness. The bovine, through its digestion, generates forces that support nervous function.

How does the bovine use these forces? They go to its head, but do not give it a big brain. This is apparent from an examination of the blood vessels. That which arises out of the cow's digestion flows to the horns (and also to the hooves). This attunes the cow's inner activity so that it supplies whatever is needed in the environment through its digestion. The cow's horn is a focal device which concentrates and redirects the forces supportive of nervous development, conserving them in the manure.

For BD 500 the horn is filled with cow manure and buried over the winter when the formative forces trickle back into the Earth in preparation for streaming outward in summer. The horn is implanted into the body of the earth almost as though it was attached to the cow, and these formative forces pour into the horn to be concentrated there. This focuses formative forces on the manure, making a potent preparation. Thus ideal forms, materials and periods are used to make a medicine to catalyze a fertile reaction.

As for the small amount used per acre, this is in keeping with the dictum of fluid dynamics that a microscopic change at a point can effect large scale changes in the medium.

Other Preps

BD 501 (horn silica) complements the BD 500. It is made by packing a cow's horn with fine quartz flour or meal and burying this in the Earth over the summer. In support of these two preps are six others, numbered BD 502 through BD 507, which are hung in the atmosphere or buried in the Earth for certain periods. They are made from yarrow flowers, chamomile flowers, stinging nettle leaves and stems, oak bark, dandelion flowers and valerian flowers. Commonly they are used to enhance compost. Moreover, a special barrel compost, made with these preps, cow manure, basalt or granite powder and finely ground eggshell, is applied like the BD 500.

Finally, there is the BD 508, the meadow horsetail preparation. Made as a decoction of *Equisetum arvense,* it is used to temper or harden plants, especially when there is excessive moisture and they might grow too watery and weak. It protects against rots and diseases, and may be used at any time to ensure a hardy farm operation.

Perspectives

Initially such medicines seem strange, but they are not mere hokum, regardless of how some dismiss them. They come from a holistic approach that has much in common with native American medicine. One might wonder if they came out of European native traditions.

Steiner grew up amongst rural Austrian peasant folk, but he indicated their native practices were lost beyond recovery. What he suggested was making a fresh start, rediscovering fundamental truths and developing new techniques.

For several centuries European religious and political leaders wanted to make themselves indispensable and have the people look to them alone for relief and salvation. Scientists as well as peasant "doctors" were the competition and were too independent and hard to control. But, peasant medicine, unlike its scientific counterpart, kept its mouth shut about its trade secrets. The tide of public opinion ran against it, and in most places witch-hunts succeeded in eliminating knowledgeable practitioners. Such a public spectacle was made of them that few chose to follow in their footsteps.

Thus the native European medicine man--exemplified by Merlin, counselor to King Arthur--fell on such hard times that so-called magic and witchcraft still have a bad reputation.

Even today, though we may start anew from a modern holistic viewpoint, repression is possible. Many biodynamic growers are reluctant to discuss their methods. The best protection, however, against those who seek to limit and control humanity is to publish the insights, knowledge and techniques of biodynamic agriculture as insurance against persecution. Nor can we afford to have these beginnings of a new agricultural science suppressed. Food production is one of the key issues in human evolution.

The Reason for BD Agriculture

When asked why people so frequently are derailed by personal ambition, illusions and petty jealousies, Steiner's response was, "This is a problem of nutrition. Nutrition as it is today does not supply the strength necessary for manifesting the spirit in physical life. A bridge can no longer be built from thinking to will and action. Food plants no longer contain the forces people need for this."

Biodynamic agriculture was his response to this need.

People who want a dogmatic belief system with teachers and authorities to do all their thinking will be disappointed with biodynamic agriculture. It is not a cookbook procedure, preserved like a fly in amber. It is dynamic and living. Times and circumstances are ever-changing, and each must be sensitive to their own unique conditions.

Chapter III

Holistic science departs radically from the prevailing analytical points of view. Goethe disagreed with Newton, not only about color, but about gravity. Newton did a convincing job of showing how gravity affected massive objects, but he completely ignored the opposite polarity, levity. Newton showed how the apple, on the dying side of its existence, fell from the tree. But, he disregarded how, on the living side of its existence, the apple got up into the tree in the first place.

Rudolf Steiner, coming from a holistic viewpoint, realized that it took both gravity and levity to fully map reality. Drawing from older European traditions that held the elements to be earth, water, air and fire, he related these to the gravitational polarity and the four states of matter--i.e., the solid liquid, gaseous and radiant states.

What, however, was the substantial nature of the radiant state? We might see the hydrogen lines in a spectroscope trained on a distant star, and say, yes, there was hydrogen. But, did any substance come from that star? Perhaps, perhaps not. The fire element stood on the brink of the insubstantial, the brink of levity.

This raised the question of levitational states analogous to the solid, liquid, gaseous and radiant states of matter. Steiner verified these calling them the ethers. Fire, since it is on the brink, is not only the least intense state of matter, but the least intense ether. This is the warmth ether, as fire is permeated by warmth. In order of intensity, the next ether, corresponding to air, he called the light ether, since air is permeated by light. Similarly, water corresponded to what he called the sound or chemical ether, and earth to the life ether.

These were not easy concepts for me. When I first encountered the word ether *in Steiner's agriculture lectures I was thrown for a loop. Having studied physics and chemistry I knew that Michelson and Morely had demonstrated that the velocity of light is independent of the velocity of the observer, thus silencing any ideas of a tangible, etheric medium as proposed in the 19th century by James Clerk Maxwell. To be sure, Paul Dirac had shown by the mid 20th century that there were mathematical reasons for accepting the existence of an abstract, intangible ether. But, this was after*

Steiner's death. Was Steiner using the discredited idea of a stationary medium? Not knowing what Steiner meant by ether was one of the stumbling blocks I had to overcome before I could grasp his recommendations for agriculture. I had to re-examine most of my scientific concepts to reach an understanding.

"The actual infinite in its highest form has created and sustains us, and in its secondary transfinite forms occurs all around us and even inhabits our minds."

— George Cantor

The Importance of Levity to Agriculture

Sir Isaac Newton succeeded admirably in focusing the attention of the scientific community on the gravitic implications of Euclidean, point-centered geometry. The mathematics of his theory of gravity were so elegant that few thought anything further worthy of consideration. Yet, only the forces governing the apple's fall were explained. It was not considered that there might be--in fact, must be--a mathematics appropriate to describe the opposite, namely levity. It was considered naive and rude to ask for an explanation of how the apple came to be in the tree.

However, for the purposes of agriculture, it is most important to ask how the apple gets up there. We need a mathematics of life. We cannot muddle through with a one-sided geometry. We need a complementary, dual system, as suggested by projective geometry, the study of all geometries.

The system taught in most schools, the Euclidean, focuses our attention upon the central, gravitic force. Its point-centered concept of space fits gravity as a field that decreases in strength as one moves outward from the center. It seems paradoxical within this framework to imagine an increase in force as one moves toward the periphery. For this opposite, dualistic concept we need a mathematical conception of space and forms that is the counterpart of point-centered geometry--a geometry of the periphery, of counterspace, of levity. The fact that such a geometry almost never is even discussed in our schools perhaps explains how modern science, in theorizing about its experiments, so often ignores the broader issues.

A Science Fair Project

For instance, it is a common science fair project to produce a vacuum in a long glass tube with a feather and a piece of lead in the bottom. By swiftly inverting the tube one can watch both the feather and the pellet fall at the same rate, arriving simultaneously. This verifies Galileo's proposal that the acceleration of freely falling bodies is the same, irrespective of their mass.

However, in everyday circumstance, due to various influences, this principle does not describe reality. Under natural conditions the feather may very well be wafted away while the lead pellet unerringly falls to the ground. This experiment does not work without a vacuum. In light of this can we call the "law of free fall" a law of nature?

We do not live in a vacuum. Rather, we experience the interaction of gravity *and* levity. It is everywhere we look, not only in volcanoes, tides and air currents, but in the growth and decay of plants and animals, the evaporation of water, the behavior of clouds and the dynamics of the universe beyond the solar system.

A New Idea

Scant attention has been paid as yet within the scientific community to the discovery in recent centuries of geometrical systems other than the Euclidean. Only in the past couple hundred years have mathematicians acknowledged that every geometric system has its opposite, dual or counterpart. Where euclidean space relates a form to a central point, counter-euclidean geometry relates this same form to the periphery. This idea has been slow to penetrate physics (although string theorists, in their search for a unified field theory, are working somewhat along these lines). Yet, the concept of mathematical duality suggests the phenomena of nature arise as an interaction between gravity and levity. We need a dual geometric system in order to explain not only how the apple falls, but how it ascends.

In fact, the geometry of counterspace has, so far, received little attention even from mathematicians. As in Galileo's day, the tendency amongst experimental scientists is to limit the study of phenomena to restricted, artificial conditions. Study in an unrestricted, open environment where natural forces interact is considered poor form.

Thus we must take the "laws" of modern science--whether they are Koch's postulates in microbiology or Newton's theories of color and gravity--with a grain of salt.

Though modern science often is accurate within the bounds it sets for itself, it is far from complete and does not take the broad view. It is inadequate to explain or predict everyday things that occur. Discoveries such as Galileo's or Newton's are valid enough within their limits, but these limits do not embrace ordinary experience.

Regardless, Goethe's concept of polarity is not really a new idea. The opposites of gravity and levity, point and periphery, earthly force and cosmic force, underlay much of what Steiner had to say about agriculture.

The Agriculture Course

Though physics and chemistry have their importance, Steiner nevertheless indicated that the most important thing for agriculture is what lies behind the physical and chemical phenomena. He pointed out that we think of ourselves as independent from the Sun, Moon, and planetary cycles that affect the Earth. These seem to have little relation to our lives, but we should not be deceived. Even though our activities may not coincide with the beginnings and endings of these heavenly cycles, they nonetheless maintain these inner rhythms. Menstruation is a case in point. However, while we are nearly emancipated, plant life is utterly dependent on these influences, and this is of the greatest importance for agriculture.

The Earth is affected by many influences, including the Moon, Mercury, Venus, Sun, Mars, Jupiter and Saturn, to say nothing of the constellations of the ecliptic. The heavenly bodies are signposts for forces which bear upon the Earth.

In the case of the distant planets, Mars, Jupiter and Saturn, their influences work through the siliceous nature, and are seen in the swellings that produce foodstuffs. In the case of the Moon, Mercury and Venus, their influences work through the limestone, and are seen in growth and reproduction.

It may seem strange to think of these heavenly bodies as most important for agriculture. After learning to think in terms of the chemical constituents, we may have little experience with the idea of forces working through the Sun, Moon and planets into life on the Earth--though we see the seasons, moonlight, clouds in the sky and apples in trees. Truly, the more we depend on explaining nature in terms of gravity and the chemical elements, the more trouble we have understanding what goes on in biodynamic agriculture.

For those who take an interest in mathematics, there is a book by George Adams and Olive Whicher, *The Plant Between Sun and Earth*. It goes into mathematical reasoning in readable fashion, and shows how the dual geometries of space and counterspace relate to the growth of plants. In the older edition, Olive Whicher's beautiful color drawings illustrate how plants manifest the gravitational and levitational opposites.

Picturing the Farm Organism

Math aside, however, growers need to know how to put these insights to work. What does this interplay between earthly and cosmic forces, gravity and levity, inner and outer planets, mean for planting corn and breeding cattle? What guidelines are there? Knowledge of soil chemistry alone is of little help. We must gain new insights.

First, Steiner compares the farm organism to the human being, and points out it is as though we were standing with our heads buried in the ground. Roots, which are beneath the Earth's surface, compare to the human head and nervous organization. Leaves and stems compare to the heart, lungs and circulation, and the flowers and fruits compare to the human sexual and metabolic organization. It is as though the farmer and his animals are running around in the belly of the farm.

Steiner goes on to say, "The farm is only healthy inasmuch as it provides its own manure from its own stock. Naturally, this will necessitate our developing a proper science of the number of animals of a given sort which we need for a given kind of farm.

"In effect," he continues, "What was said at the beginning-- describing that which is above the Earth's surface as a kind of belly, and that which is beneath as a kind of head-existence--is not complete unless we also understand the animal organism in this way. The animal organism lives in the whole complex of Nature's household. In form and color and configuration, and in the structure and consistency of its substance from the front to the hinder parts, it is related to these influences: From the snout towards the heart, the Saturn, Jupiter and Mars influences are at work; in the heart itself the Sun; and behind the heart, towards the tail, the Venus, Mercury and Moon influences. In this respect, those who are interested in these matters should develop their knowledge above all by learning to *read the form*. To be able to do this is of very great importance."

Maria Thun

Maria Thun, a European biodynamic researcher, has concentrated on reading the forms, especially those of plants, and correlating her observations with the positions, cycles and relationships of the Sun, Moon and planets against the starry background. By repetitive daily plantings of selected vegetables over a period of years with careful observations and records, she found consistent relationships between vegetable characteristics and planting times. Moreover, she discovered that plantings made at the Moon's nodes, and at occultations or eclipses, frequently suffered from damping off and diseases. Thus she not only worked out which times were best for different types of crops, but also found there were times to avoid planting.

According to her research, leaf crops should be planted when the Moon is in water--the constellations of Cancer, Scorpio or Pisces. For roots the Moon should be in earth--Capricorn, Taurus or Virgo. Flowers prefer air--Libra, Aquarius and Gemini. And for fruits and grains the fire constellations of Aries, Leo and Sagittarius were best.

Researchers with low organic matter soils, dependent on chemical inputs, may have trouble duplicating her research as she found that where the soil is rich with humus these relationships are far stronger.

Interestingly her research showed that plants respond to the positions of the actual constellations. Tropical astrology, which is commonly used for casting peoples' horoscopes, divides the ecliptic into twelve signs of thirty degrees each, calling the beginning of spring (the vernal equinox) zero degrees Aries. In the time of

Ptolemy (approximately 130 A.D.) zero degrees Aries was indeed where the Sun crossed the equator in the spring. Now, however, due to the precession of the equinoxes, the vernal equinox falls roughly thirty degrees away on the cusp between the constellations of Pisces and Aquarius. In other words, tropical astrologers are more than two thousand years out of date. Consequently tropical astrology, although it is a holistic system, is not representative of the actual heavenly picture.

Biodynamic Calendars

Maria Thun developed a sowing calendar for biodynamic growers. It was based on sidereal astrology, which relates to the present day stars and constellations. It provided systematic guidelines for when to plant and cultivate. Two such calendars are available for English speaking farmers. The Thun calendar, *Working With The Stars,* is available from BD Preps in Woolwine, Virginia, and *The Kimberton Hills Agricultural Calendar* is available from Kimberton, Pennsylvania. (See appendix for addresses.)

Much remains to be learned about the interaction of gravity and levity. As we develop knowledge by reading the form, we can establish a true science for working with nature so that we know what are the best ways to farm.

BD preparation maker Hugh Courtney stirs a portion of BD 507 as the last step in kicking off some BD barrel compost. Applied at the rate of a quarter cup per acre, barrel compost often is the first BD treatment used on new land.

Chapter IV

In the early days of setting up Union Agricultural Institute (UAI) I worked off the farm in order to pay the bills. I trucked produce for a tomato repacking firm. Then I went to work for a dairy near the Institute. Neither job paid much money, though they were good experience.

On a trip to Louisiana I got a job as an oilfield cook. This had me home one week out of four. When the price of oil dropped and drilling activity slowed, I got on as a carpenter building highway bridges in Atlanta. I was home only on Saturdays and Sundays. During the week I planned what to do on the farm. Both the oilfield and the bridge job required that on the farm I find what produced the best result for the least effort. I also had time to think about what really occurred in nature. When I was home I paid attention and observed, and I began to see beyond my preconceived ideas.

Things happened that the standard ways of thinking failed to explain. The more I used the BD preps, and the less I worried about the advice of conventional thinkers, the more successful my farming became.

I realize how it sounds.

"You what? You spend an hour stirring a crock of springwater with an ounce of bull dung in it, and then sprinkle it on with a big wallpaper brush like the archbishop anointing the crowds? Sure, I know what that is. Superstitious magic. No! No! Sympathetic magic! It is superstitious! Are you sure you're all right? You don't need to see a shrink?"

Nevertheless, I am as skeptical as the next person. I question all theories. But, I am skeptical even of skepticism. I do not discard a notion just because I cannot make sense of it right away. I try to give new ideas a chance.

The BD preps required little effort, were completely non-toxic, and with them the soil turned brown and crumbly. Seeds caught hold and grew with vigor. Not bad.

While farming was my dream, it got only a fourth of my time. I needed good results, cheap. The BD preps were made to order.

Gradually I sorted things out and started correcting my early blunders.

Toward the end of my bridge building career, where I stayed during the week in southwest Atlanta, I had a residential city lot to test my methods on. This was a site unscathed, or at least it was scathed only by pollution and urban development.

"Daylight is the condition of things polarized within the master vortex. Night is manufactured by the earth coming betwixt the master's focus and the outer extreme . . . so that both night and day continue all the time, and we realize them both alternately in consequence of the axial motion of the earth. As in the case of night or of any darkness, when the needles of atmospheric substance are disturbed in polarity, or when the lines of needles are cut, as in eclipse, there is no direct manifestation of the earth's vortexian currents, and such is the cause of darkness. For which reason nitrogenous plants grow rapidly at night, whilst the ripening of certain fruits and grains require the light of day. For by this vortexya are seeds and grains and fruits and herbs charged with it. Whereof when men eateth, or--as in breathing air--these things go into dissolution, as hereinafter mentioned, the heat is eliminated, and lodgeth itself in man."

-OAHSPE, Book of Cosmogeny and Prophecy

Starting From Scratch

During the early part of 1985 I worked on a bridge complex in Marietta, near Atlanta. My co-worker, Adama, rented me her basement, and with it the yard.

The back yard was shaded, but with a few spots where the soil was decent. The front yard had been bulldozed, was steep, with hard-packed red clay and hardly anything living, even an ant. It barely supported a few tufts of grass and some scraggly bushes.

Starting the Project

On the positive side, the lot was nearly an acre. The house sat on the hilltop a little back from the middle, and the front slope caught good sun. There was nearly two thirds of a ton of compost which I had started the previous year for Adama with a truckload of oak and poplar bark and some cow manure.

Back when I first built the pile I used Dr. Pfeiffer's Quick Composting Compound, which contained the BD preps. But, for several months no earthworms appeared. I began to suspect none were in the area. Finally I brought a jar of earthworms to Atlanta from Blairsville, and that got the pile working.

Adama and I worked forty to fifty hours a week, and our jobs were not easy. Monday morning I would pick her up and drive to work. We got back close to dark. We both fixed meals and she had her three-year-old son to take care of. Usually I washed the sawdust and concrete off and worked at my typewriter. I did not have much energy for the yard.

Then it was up again at five for another day of bridge construction. My paycheck barely met the bills at the Institute. Fridays, after I dropped Adama off, I headed back to Blairsville, 125 miles away.

So, there was little money or energy to put into the yard, but I wanted to see what I could do. My biggest advantage was having tools, seeds, plants and animals, as well as knowing where the cheapest materials were.

The first thing I brought down was eighteen bales of old hay, cut late and full of seeds. Not good feed hay, but just the thing to mulch a barren hillside.

Then I brought my mower to town, though scarcely anything needed mowing besides some vines near the borders and one lush patch near the water meter. Working in the evening just before dark, I stirred and sprayed a one acre unit of barrel compost and sowed rye, wheat, crimson clover and sweet clover into the scattered mulch of hay. The following week I applied BD 500, and a few weeks later, BD 50l.

Encouraging Life

Near the house where the slope was gentle, I marked off four little forty-inch-wide beds following the contour. I put the compost from the backyard pile on the lower two beds, and dusted the other two with wood ashes.

The soil was hard to dig. I spent twelve hours and barely did an adequate job. Double digging was out of the question.

Wanting to get more of an earthworm reservoir established in the front yard and put some life in the soil, I brought some wormy compost from Blairsville and scattered it around the scraggly azaleas up against the house. Then I mulched the bushes with bags of oak leaves off the street. Acorns in the leaves attracted a family of squirrels which worked the mulch over, and manured it.

I scattered sunflower seeds on the hillside for the birds to eat, and shredded leaves with the lawnmower to start another compost pile. In the back yard I planted bamboo as well as peppermint, stinging nettle and comfrey patches. In the more promising spots I planted daffodils, irises and other flowers.

I took two soil samples, one from the beds that got the compost, and one from the mulched hillside. The slope, with the grains and clovers, had a pH of 4.8 and low fertility in every category except potassium. The beds with the compost had a pH of 5.8 and somewhat more nutrients.

For boron, which was deficient, I dusted a half box of borax on the front yard for a first application. The slope needed dolomitic lime and I had an old pile on the farm, so I scraped up a couple hundred pounds to scatter on the worst areas.

The Doves

A flock of doves found the wheat and rye seed under the mulch, eating it and manuring. I had to sow it down twice more before there was enough growing to make a stand.

In the composted beds I planted potatoes, onions, garlic, spinach, lettuce and beets, and in the wood ashed beds I planted peas.

This may sound like a lot of work, but I had my priorities in order and I averaged only thirty minutes or so after work three or four days a week. The biggest chore was digging the beds, which I did on a day when work was called off on the bridge. My only real error was building the new compost pile in the back yard where the previous one had been, requiring more wheelbarrowing.

I had a couple stands of bees in Blairsville, and I brought one down for the garden. I also brought a couple of rabbit hutches, with rabbits, to provide manure for compost piles.

The potatoes did well. They also bloomed, setting little green fruits full of seeds, which I collected to grow out the next year. The onions and lettuce were small, but they were perfectly healthy. The peas were truly superior with incredibly sweet pods. Tomatoes of every kind volunteered, along with a couple huge watermelons.

The rye on the slope grew to nearly eighteen inches by May, and it made three or four seeds to the head. This was pitiful, but, in all fairness, it was a tenfold improvement over the sparse grass of the year before. The clover germinated and grew, but it was dwarfed, except in the most heavily limed areas.

At the end of April the bridge job was finished and we were laid off. I visited only occasionally. In June I sowed buckwheat and soybeans on the slope, mowing off the rye. The doves ate almost all the soybeans and half the buckwheat. The remaining buckwheat grew to sixteen inches and, like the rye, made three or four grains per stalk. I mixed up another batch of soybeans, popcorn and mud, hoping to baffle the doves. They ate most of the popcorn, but the soybeans sprouted and grew. Along with the soybeans a volunteer crop of ragweed took over, getting a little nitrogen from the soybeans, which were inoculated with *Rhizobium japonicum*, for nitrogen fixation. The ragweed reached six feet tall and bloomed in September. Of course, I sprayed BD preps, applying them four times during this period.

With the ragweeds so tall I could envision the progress made underground by their roots. The soil started to loosen up.

I brought a truckload of quarry dust from Blairsville in September, and sowed rye, sweet clover, turnips and rape along with various odds and ends. I mowed everything flat, broadcasting the quarry dust on top to sift down through the mulch, and spraying everything down again with BD preps. Rain gave me a break, and the seeds sprouted before the doves could eat them. The former desert became the greenest yard on Avon street.

The bee hive made four gallons of honey, and the fall collards at the top of the hill--where the peas had been--were tiny, but good. The turnips in the rye cover on the hillside got no bigger than my thumb. The fall celery and spinach were also a disappointment. But, it was not bad for a first-year garden in a former barren waste. At least everything survived and grew, even the herbs, daffodils, irises, and bamboo.

On the Way

In 1986 I visited Adama in March and planted potatoes, peas, onions, and collards, changing locations in the beds. Where previously it had taken twelve hours to dig the beds, now it took only two. The compost pile, however, was again inadequate. To remedy this I brought pickup loads of quarry dust, oak bark and commercial laying house manure from Blairsville, making a compost pile at the top of the garden.

In April much of the slope was still acid and poor, so I brought nine hundred pounds of lime from Blairsville along with a couple bushels of compost. This evened out the growth of the rye and clover so that by the end of May there was a four foot high, waving field with full heads of grain.

In early June I brought another bee colony down, dividing hives and taking the divisions back to Blairsville for two weeks so the colonies would stay separated. I mowed the rye down on top of a broadcast sowing of Laredo soybeans, a hay variety. I also scattered a couple handfuls of pumpkin seeds, and without any tillage I laid out rows of corn in the stubble across the contour of the slope. On top of the corn seed I mounded strips of compost an inch or two high and five or six inches wide.

Everything came up. Of course, it helped that the rye mulch was a quarter of an inch deep. A soil test showed the pH of the slope was up to 5.2, and fertility levels had more than doubled in every department except potassium, which was already good.

A Cosmic Pipe and Basic "H"

I planted a homemade version of Galen Hieronymus' Cosmic Pipe, built on a design Paul Esch of Douglasville, Georgia gave me. This is a device used to broadcast environmental energies, and I used it to strengthen the effects of my biodynamic preparations.

I also sprayed the whole front slope down with a dilute solution of Shaklee's Basic "H" to help flush toxins out of the soil since the slope faced a busy thoroughfare. Basic "H" reduces the surface tension of water, making it "wetter," and I believed this would also assure better access to minerals for the plants.

But, it was dry, and the topsoil was still very thin. Adama had to water to get the growth started.

The soybeans formed an ocean of vines. The corn and bean thinnings made good rabbit feed. The pumpkins grew huge vines, though their fruits did not mature before I sowed and mowed my rye, clover, turnip and rape mixture again in early September. The corn got six feet tall and made respectable ears, which the rabbits enjoyed.

There was only one problem. The jungle of growth proved a haven for neighborhood rats, and two separate attempts to get male cats to make this home failed. This led to planting the winter cover crop and mowing the corn and soybeans in early September, as rats were not welcome members of the ecology.

Success

This time the no-till rye, clover, turnip and rape grew luxuriantly. The turnips were big as my fist and sweeter even than on the farm in Blairsville.

The corn and soybean clippings made more than half an inch of mulch. Where the latest pea patch was, I planted celery, broccoli and cabbages, in order to rotate from soil building legumes to heavy feeding leaf crops. I built new hutches for the rabbits, which had matured and needed separation. The turnip and rape yields in the no-till rye on the slope were each nearly five bushels. The bees spent their efforts drawing out comb wax in their new boxes, and since it takes nine pounds of honey to make one pound of wax there was no honey crop.

From the original backyard compost site Adama and I moved four volunteer peach trees out to the edge of the front slope near the bees. An especially good volunteer apple tree was left to become permanent at the end of one of the beds. A December soil test showed the pH was 6.5 and fertility was high across the board. Earthworms were everywhere, and my soil sampling tool was easy to push into the ground. The rich, green color of the rye showed the benefits of the preceding blanket of soybeans.

The waving field of grain on the once barren slope was utterly no-till, as all I had done was plant, sow, mow, spray BD preps and spread a little compost, lime, granite and borax. I question if cultivation could have done as much. What two years previously had been the poorest yard on Avon street was now the most fertile.

Chickens scratch in the rich, fresh-tilled soil at UAI, a Georgia biodynamic farm. Although use of the BD preps accounts somewhat for this pale red clay's transformation into rich, brown, crumbly loam, biodynamic practices go further. Biodynamic farmers try to produce all their own composts by raising their own livestock and feeds, as well as making use of such practices as mixed plantings, strip cropping and crop rotation that help to ensure the widest diversity of species within the ecology.

Chapter V

The following story about no-till cropping without chemicals ran in the April 1988 Acres, U.S.A.

I would like to experiment on a larger scale growing crops without tillage and without chemicals, while making compost by feeding these crops to animals. Especially in the southeast, farmers are faced with the necessity of building soil. My experiments showed I spent the least time and built the most topsoil no-tilling corn and soybeans rotated with no-till winter plantings of rye and legumes such as vetch or crimson clover.

Also I found that the old idea that one's fields should be meticulously weed free, growing only one kind of plant, should be questioned. It looks impressive, but frequently deals death to the ecology, leading to dependence upon purchased inputs.

Moreover, there needs to be an alternative to government research, which has increased growers' toxic burdens by pushing chemical no-till cropping. Of course, government research also gives impetus to changing the notions farmers have about how their fields should look. At least it dispensed with the fresh plowed look, and staunched somewhat the wounds in the Earth's skin through which her life force was bleeding away.

"The truth is the one thing that nobody will believe."

–George Bernard Shaw

No-Till Farming without Chemicals

In the sixties it became clear that topsoil losses with standard tillage practices were leading to agricultural collapse. The political and economic winds pointed research toward a revision of tillage practices.

Research Hiatus

The people doing research were of high social standing, and were pillars of their communities. They were calm, intelligent, reasonable, and the backbone of our society, even in our troubled times. They needed a way out of an impasse, and they saw what could be done.

Chemical no-till farming was introduced. You could not erode unplowed land. That was sensible. But, their funding was for chemical research, so they could not carry no-till methods to the full and natural conclusion of maximizing both biomass production and digestive activity. It was more expedient to increase the use of fertilizers, herbicides and insecticides. They could not eschew the chemicals which killed the ants, spiders, beetles, moles, worms, flies, pillbugs, centipedes, springtails and mites that riddled, honeycombed and fertilized, and through their intricate interaction provided the abundant air necessary for superior root growth. With heavy machinery packing the soil, where was the air going to come from for healthy root zone action?

The effect of the chemical blitzkrieg on soil fauna could not be addressed by the "hard-ball" researchers. This means that after three or four years of no-till a field is usually so hard packed it has to be plowed.

Permaculture, organic and biodynamic researchers could investigate no-till farming without chemicals. They could not be de-funded, unfunded or unrefunded--not altogether. But, they could be out-market researched, out-published and out-sales forced, and they were. Chemical industries with billions of dollars in annual sales saw to that, protecting their profits even if these came at the expense of the long range survival of the human species.

People like Masanobu Fukuoka or Bill Mollison could be tolerated because they were unlikely to get big farmers, let alone farm corporations, to follow as long as their methods were relegated to the fringes. Advertising, funded research and publishing could manage this. Better farming techniques were of little concern as long as they did not get the right coverage.

I knew this well enough from participating in the process. I not only studied psychology and market research, but I worked on press crews running off those beautiful four-color-process jobs for *Prairie Farmer* and *Wallace's Farmer*. Who cared if marketing psychology spelled the doom of the species a hundred years down the road? Worry about that when we get to it, if we do. We have to pay the rent and buy groceries today.

On The Fringes

And so, out on the fringes, scattered independents tried things they thought might work despite the propaganda. One soybean/wheat rotation in Georgia involved drilling soybeans no-till into the stubble right behind the wheat combine. In the fall, when the frost hit the soybean leaves, wheat was broadcast from the air. By the time the beans were combined a young stand of wheat was established. When the wheat was combined and the soybeans drilled again, the soil organic matter had increased.

Experience showed few weed problems. Because the soybean seed is so large and packs such sprouting power, it need only be drilled in the wheat stubble with the right spacing to smother most of its competition.

Likewise the timing of planting the wheat so that the soy leaves fell on top of it, and the relative winter hardiness of the grain crop, put its competition out of the running too. But, some interesting problems can occur.

For instance, one farmer in Georgia using this rotation found the organic matter built up so thickly on the surface after a few years that his machinery could not plug the beans through the accumulated crop residues into the soil. This was a problem because soybeans need good soil contact with sufficient moisture to sprout, and Georgia summers can be quite dry at times. The mulch buildup could not be relied on to supply the necessary moisture to each seed. Still, many a Georgia farmer would like to have so much organic matter in his fields.

This farmer had to plow to bury his organic matter because he had too much--too much biomass and not enough digestive activity. He did not have enough animal life in the soil. An editor of a farm paper laughed when telling me about this, though it failed to get proper attention in his publication. The question that should have been asked was why there was so little digestive activity in the soil, and how to increase it.

No-Till Rotations

In Japan, Masanobu Fukuoka perfected a method of rotating rice and barley (summer and winter grain crops) in a clover sod, planted no-till without any chemicals. I have not experimented with his rice scheme, though a few others around the country are applying these ideas to large scale rice production.

Instead I have run no-till trials of corn with soybeans, and rye with clover or vetch, in summer/winter rotations. I am not prepared to grow rice, and Georgia is different from Japan. I do not strive for pure stands, as with them soil animals do not seem to work so enthusiastically to build soil.

The corn/soybean leg of my rotation gets what compost I can spare, especially if the soil is poor. I let volunteer weeds be. Experience shows that in good soil the annual grain and legume covers do a good job of suppressing weeds without herbicides. I found that cutting (or grazing) off the stubble close allows permanent legumes, like alfalfa and red clover, to bounce back rapidly, forestalling the emergence of weeds, while the grains, which tend to sprout more slowly, come up through these legumes and do just fine.

Test and Select

Farmers must test and select the best crop varieties for their rotations. For instance, popcorn was simply too slow getting up through alfalfa re-growth to make a stand. Alfalfa really comes back fast. But my 15-foot-tall open-pollinated field corn varieties have always put it into high gear in alfalfa.

Sowing the new crop and mowing or grazing down the standing growth (or haying or ensiling it) seems to be an economical means of building organic matter. As long as soil fauna are encouraged, both active leaf surface and digestive activity appear to be maximized with annual crops without tillage. This increases soil fertility without going off the farm.

I would apply biodynamic preparations, composts, rock powders, and whatever major or minor nutrient supplements are needed to get the land into thriving condition. On a new field to get the fertility up in the beginning I would unhesitatingly use something like Leland Taylor's (see Agronics, Inc. in appendix I) Fertimax program, which supplies sufficient of all the major and minor nutrients in a humus based substrate. Radionic field units, when skillfully used, can also be of considerable assistance, as both crops and soil fauna respond enthusiastically to subtle energies when these are properly applied.

Also, I have found top dressing with crushed granite from my local gravel quarry to be valuable in stimulating earthworms, as they are like chickens. They have no teeth and need small pieces of stone grit to grind up what they eat. In living soil these critters scarf up the crushed stone particles lying on the surface and carry them into the soil with little delay.

The moral of this story is that farmers might do better attending to what is going on in the fringes.

The careful, sincere, mainline agricultural researchers--solid folks though they are--are bound and gagged. They are not likely to research and publish what goes against the economic powers. They dare not conflict with Monsanto or Dow or the Wall Street investors.

"Of course," they say, "You cannot no-till without herbicides."

They understand well enough. They have to pay rent and buy groceries today. Let humanity pay the bill further down the road.

Naturally, it is time for the giants of world finance to realize their collective financial, scientific and political follies and to back off from the planetary profit-taking presently proceeding in the name of progress. But they have to do this *en masse*. Otherwise the ones who exercise restraint may be swallowed by those who do not.

BD 500, also called horn manure, being buried for the winter season.

Chapter VI

This chapter combines two articles dealing with fertilizers. "The Cheapest Fertilizer In Georgia" ran in 1987 in Acres U.S.A. *"Raw Manure" ran in* Biological Farming News *in 1988. Both are of importance for those trying to farm biodynamically.*

Many believe they must have special stone powders which come from far away and are expensive. Others think any kind of material that corrects for low pH is acceptable. Moreover, the necessity of composting manures is not widely recognized, especially in academic circles.

One of the tenets of biodynamic agriculture is that any imported fertilizer is a remedy for an ailing farm. A truly healthy farm needs no outside inputs. In today's world healthy farms are rare. Until this situation is corrected, many will need to import various fertilizer materials.

Most farms regularly bring in lime and chemical fertilizers. Organic farms often import manures, greensand, colloidal phosphates, powdered limestone, foliar seaweed, or fossil humus materials. Any of these may be excellent inputs, but too often the reasons for choosing one fertilizer over another amount to guesswork. Even those who do a good job of soil testing and fertilization suffer from materialistic thinking without adequate concepts of force. For instance, because silica is present in virtually all soils, its activation as the carrier of cosmic forces is almost always ignored.

By comparison to chemical fertilizers, high quality organic and powdered rock fertilizers usually analyze low in nitrogen, phosphorus and potassium, but yield better long range results for the money. One such material, granite dust, is plentiful in my locality. It is inexpensive, and for the most part it has replaced lime, colloidal phosphate, wood ashes, and other mineral sources in my farming operation. It contains little if any nitrogen, but analyses around 4% potassium, 0.75% phosphorus, and has enough calcium (nearly 3%) to draw nitrogen into well-aerated, humusy soils. Moreover, its silica content (27%) is one of its most beneficial characteristics. One hardly hears about silica, but biodynamic growers know it to be one of the two most important minerals.

More than anything, though, we should think of materials as carriers of forces. Forces constantly impinge upon materials, and their functions unfold over time. It is not good science to ignore the forces and functions inherent in living soils with their flora and fauna. Just analyzing the mineral content of an earthworm, for instance, does not do it justice. It takes more than minerals to make life, purpose and personality. Nourishing these is what agriculture is all about.

Part of this chapter deals with manure and why it should be composted. Manure should not be applied raw unless spread very thinly on the surface.

Reductionists look at the volatilization of ammonia and leaching of nitrates that can occur when manures break down. They remonstrate that not only does composting take time, it wastes nitrogen. While they may not be the best compost makers to begin with, they ignore the nitrogen fixing capacity of good compost, its high populations of Azotobacters and the implications this has for a healthy astrality. They also ignore the function of oxygen and its importance for healthy etheric force. Among other things, oxygen has profound effects on the kinds and populations of favorable versus pathogenic microorganisms in most soils. And, this is just the beginning.

Subtle organic chemistry is given nowhere near enough consideration. Biological transmutation is not investigated. The deposition of airborne dusts on the land receives no attention at all. Future investigations should address these lacks. But, at the very least we should consider rock powders and composts.

"It is said that there are two ways of looking at everything. That is true and less than true, for there are many ways. Some of them are good ways and some are bad."

–Robert A. Heinlein

The Cheapest Fertilizer in Georgia

Georgia's precambrian soils are some of the world's oldest. They have endured millennia of heavy rainfall in a warm environment, and are weathered and depleted.

An ecological grower has a tough time raising top quality crops on such soils. In many cases the accessible reserves of both major and minor nutrients have been exhausted. This means Georgia soils tend to be poorer than Iowa's or Oregon's for growing easily-stressed crops, breeding livestock, or raising quality seed. For instance, Georgia lettuce is rare in supermarkets while California lettuce is common. And, prior to widespread application of limestone, it was customary to raise hogs in Georgia rather than cattle since hogs fare better on starved soils.

Liming

Customarily growers are (incorrectly) told they should lime to raise their pH. Low pH (high acidity) means the soil cupboard is bare and needs restocking.

Lime is a term commonly used to indicate calcium and magnesium carbonates. On the average, organisms need eight to ten times as much calcium as magnesium and three to four times as much magnesium as potassium. This means calcium is needed more than any other element to restore most exhausted soils, and applying powdered limestone frequently gives a good response.

Thinking that one limes to raise pH, however, leads to applying lime with no regard for achieving optimum levels of major and minor nutrients. Just applying any kind of lime simply to neutralize acidity may not result in balanced nutrients within the root zone. Many soils are high in magnesium, but deficient in calcium, and need calcitic lime. A few, such as mine in Georgia, are deficient in magnesium and need dolomitic lime.

Liming does raise the pH. High pH means the soil storehouse is full. Too bad if it is full of the wrong minerals. That is not much easier to correct than too much salt in the soup.

Alternatives To Liming

Broadly speaking, limestone is a sedimentary rock. Limestone deposits were laid down after most basaltic and granitic soils were formed. However, as soils weather, more than just calcium and magnesium are lost. A wide variety of nutrients must be returned to restore such a soil. To this end basalt or granite dusts may be better sources of minerals than powdered limestones, as they are more balanced soil building materials.

The Cheapest Fertilizer in Georgia/ Raw Manure   73

Testing

Not all soils are the same, nor are all basaltic or granitic formations. For example, siliceous materials such as quartz or feldspar may form a high percentage of the total mineral content in granites. Alternatively oxides, sulfides and other metallic compounds may predominate. Ideally tests should be conducted on both soils and rock powders to assure a good match. Moreover, dynamic factors such as particle sizes and etheric force are fully as important as substances. For instance, a fairly good rule of thumb is that the more paramagnetic a rock powder is, the more likely it is to be a useful fertilizer for building etheric force, especially if cultivation leaves crop residues on the surface. (As it should, see orgonomy.)

A quantitative laboratory test for fifty or more elements can be cost-prohibitive. It is unlikely that any but larger growers can go this route. Dowsing and radionic analysis, which are qualitative tests, can be cheaper. Allowing livestock access to a rock powder to see if they like to eat it is another inexpensive test. If they eat it there is a good chance it is needed. Small scale field applications of rock powders probably are the simplest and cheapest tests of all.

As a general rule, after preliminary examination of soil needs and rock powder contents, if a grower thinks a thing beneficial, he can try a little, observe the results and determine whether to use more. This kind of testing anyone can do.

Highlights From The Literature

Donald Weaver and John D. Hamaker wrote a book about rock powders entitled *The Survival of Civilization.* Another good book on this subject is Julius Henshel's *Bread From Stones.*

Studies were made in Georgia during the fifties that analyzed rock dusts from Florida to Vermont. In general, these granite and gneiss dusts contained over 25% silicon, about 4% potassium, roughly 0.5 to 0.7% phosphorous, and trace amounts of all the minor nutrient elements. Although calcium and magnesium were not quite as high as those in need of lime might desire, sulfur, iron, manganese and other micronutrients were present in good proportions.

In general my local quarry dust contained all the minerals my soils needed with the exception that copper and boron were not adequate and had to be supplemented with trace mineral applications.

Field Trials

I made extensive field trials of the dusts from two local quarries. Analysis showed one contained a higher proportion of phosphorus, while the other contained more magnesium. But, the differences were not great. The main question was how much I should apply.

A highly organic (not merely carbonaceous, but protoplasmic) soil has a large capacity to absorb and exchange nutrients. Such soils can absorb heavy applications of stone powders. Sandy soils are the least absorptive, with clay soils in between. A sandy soil may absorb only one to three tons per acre of such rock powder in raising the pH from 5 to 6.5, whereas a highly protoplasmic soil may absorb as much as twenty tons per acre for the same change in pH.

In my trials, alfalfa, clovers, beans and peas gave excellent responses to heavy applications of my local rock powder, as rock dusts, in general, are noted for their ability to assist in drawing nitrogen into the soil. However, most vegetables such as corn, potatoes, onions, cabbages and lettuce yielded better when the rock powder was incorporated into composts at a rate of not more than ten percent or less of the total weight. Composting not only buffered the rock dusts, but it provided the capacity to hold and exchange nutrients. Root crops, such as radishes, carrots and beets, all did poorly with direct applications and were best when left unfertilized.

Of course, even today when I put new land into production on my farm I also use powdered dolomitic lime, copper sulfate, borax or borates. Especially in the midwest, however, soils are loaded with magnesium, and dolomite should be avoided. Calcitic lime should be used instead. This illustrates the need for tailoring applications to each specific soil.

Locating a Source

Transportation is the chief cost of stone powders. It is important to find local sources.

Quarries must submit samples for analysis before crushing gravel for public use. Usually this is protection against releasing toxic minerals. Growers should investigate in order to avoid problems.

Since dusts collect rapidly at most rock crushers, many quarries will give this material away or sell it cheaply. In some cases dump truck or spreader truck loads may be obtained. Where gravel is washed, settling ponds also collect rock sediments. Although some leaching of nutrients may occur in these ponds, such deposits are rich sources of minerals.

Comparisons

Compared to chemicals, granitic or basaltic quarry dusts are long lasting, slow release fertilizers. Often this is just what farmers need. On a living soil with balanced vegetation, microorganisms and earthworms, $5.50 worth of my local quarry dust gives me a slow release supply of forty to fifty dollars worth of phosphorous and potassium, to say nothing of the lime, silica and other trace minerals.

I might add that I was unable to grow quality lettuce in Georgia until I used my local quarry dust to balance my fertilization program.

"Intelligence is the true manure."

–Osawagu

Raw Manure

Manure is one of the best things to return to the soil. But, to incorporate manure raw into the soil is an error. Before manure is applied it should be composted.

Fukuoka

Masanobu Fukuoka says he does not compost his chickens' manure and he gets good results. This is because he lets his chickens range freely, manuring in widely scattered small quantities. When he scoops up manures from collection sites he scatters this very thinly. He does no plowing or other cultivation, letting earthworms, beetles, ants, etc. work the manure into the soil. This imitates nature, so it works quite well. It does not incorporate manure into the soil raw.

On a living pasture, dung beetles mix soil into the manure droppings, helping them compost. In a couple months few traces are left of the manure. It is composted.

On the other hand, where manure collects, care must be taken to ensure proper composting. By controlling the composting process, mature digestive activity is aided and the soil is enlivened. This works on the soil and releases minerals that were previously unavailable.

Results of Raw Manure

If one puts manure on, incorporating it raw into the soil, several undesirable things result. (1) Manure requires oxygen to break down into plant food. The more deeply it is incorporated, the less oxygen there is. Oxygen deficiency means anaerobic breakdown, which favors plant diseases. (2) Volatile nitrogen (ammonia) and soluble nitrogen (primarily nitrates) are produced by the breakdown of manure in the soil. If these are present in quantity, they stifle or burn the fine feeder roots of crop plants. Since weeds often can tolerate more abuse than crop plants, this condition favors weeds, especially the tall ones. (3) Soluble nitrogen compounds leach into the water table and lower water quality. (4) Due to the presence of harmful microorganisms, raw manure fed crops tend to spoil more quickly and to taste bad. There also is the potential for harboring parasites. Produce handlers usually will not buy crops if they know they have been fertilized with raw manure. (5) As with crops fertilized with nitrogen salts, raw manure fed crops will be pumped up with nitrogen, but will tend to be low in sugar and deficient in silicon, calcium and other important "hard" nutrients. This makes them subject to insect attack.

Worse than the Chemicals

Raw manure tends to produce sicker plants than salt fertilization, despite adding organic matter and micronutrient factors to the soil.

My experience shows that deep incorporation of raw manure in large quantities can cause toxic soil conditions that persist for years. Subsoiling may help cure these problems by getting oxygen down to the toxic zones, but it is better not to cause such problems in the first place.

Manures also tend to contain all the poisons used commercially in producing animal feeds, plus all the chemicals, antibiotics, metallic salts, and pharmaceuticals used in the animal confinement operation. Some manures may be quite poisonous. I know from importing other farmers' manure problems and plowing them under deep. I had tall, weak-stemmed, diseased, insect-ridden crops that lost the battle with weeds. Radionic testing revealed traces of DDT, malathion and parathion in my soils and my water table.

To summarize, the use of raw manure can result in: (1) Oxygen deficiencies and anaerobic conditions. (2) Root burn on crop plants and severe weed problems. (3) Pollution of the soil and water table. (4) The proliferation of parasites and disease-causing microorganisms and (5) Severe insect infestations.

Knowing What I Know Now

I would advise that *everything* be composted prior to incorporation into the soil. This decreases oxygen demand, stabilizes nitrogen, eliminates parasites and pathogens and grows healthier crops. Ideally farms should produce their own manures and compost them, thus avoiding toxic inputs. Until a farm is thriving, fertilizer may need to be brought in. But, rather than use other farmers' toxic manures, one might import clean feeds, good quality compost or geologically concentrated humus such as Leland Taylor's Fertimax. Had I done this at the beginning instead of importing raw manures, I would have avoided these problems.

Also, though biodynamic preparations are effective in balancing and cleaning the environment, my experience indicates that they do a better job where they do not have to overcome the effects of fertilizing with raw manure.

Chapter VII

I have often been asked, "What should I do first? Where do I start?"

I doubt there is a formula, as in baking or chemistry. Everyone has a different starting point and a different path. In general, however, it boils down to observing where one is and going from there, step by step, toward one's goals. Long term goals simply take a lot of steps.

While this sounds straightforward, there often are obstacles. Everyone has blind spots, and these impediments must be recognized to be removed. Clarity--unobstructedness--cannot be achieved until prejudices and misconceptions are swept aside. This is easier said than done, as clearing up mistaken ideas often involves painful experience. Doubtless we learn more from our mistakes than from our successes.

It is at the level of sub-conscious emotion that our prejudices come into play, and it is there that we find our obstacles.

In looking at a field that has weeds amongst the corn, do we feel, "What a careless farmer that must be!" Are we thinking only in terms of the number of bushels of corn it will yield? Are diversity, sustainability, environmental health and freedom from inputs ignored in the rush to judgment? Do we have to impoverish our farm ecologies before we are ready to open our eyes?

It is common to believe only what carries the imprimatur of authority. This is the basis of true belief, but it is not the path of discovery. The truth is stranger than any descriptions of it. Inevitably it goes beyond our theories or beliefs. If we want to learn, we have to seek knowledge, question authority and think for ourselves. If at the emotional level we fear this, we have a problem. Sooner or later painful experience will force us to open our eyes.

Most schools today demand true belief. They present theories and explanations as facts that must be memorized and recited. Somehow educators have lost sight of the root of the word, educate (educare, which means to draw out). This is an indication that our society is headed for trouble.

The Meanings of Words   79

In school I was told I must study. However, there were no courses in study. There was not even a convincing definition of it. Study should result in realization and understanding. It cannot be memorization or enforcement of rote procedure. It must be a process of thinking and examination until understanding results. The best way I know of to eliminate preconceptions, misconceptions and blind spots is to examine something and think about it from different viewpoints. Removing these obstacles paves the way for cognition.

"You made an important decision today, my brother, on the spiritual side," Osawagu stated matter-of-factly. "Do you remember what it was?"

"I hope I didn't," I responded. "I try not to make decisions; it is so limiting. I try to come to realizations instead."

Osawagu cocked his head ever so slightly to the side and managed to convey a look which seemed to say, 'Very well, I grasp that all right. Now let me present that question again. Give me another answer.'

"You mean when I mentioned I thought it particularly astute earlier when you said that we must establish a science which is not based on postulates."

"That is what I mean, my brother."

"The postulates can be called axioms and it makes no difference; science makes little progress in that direction," I ventured.

"It makes no difference what they are called," Osawagu nodded, smiling. "They have no referent."

"No stable datum," I agreed.

"Precisely."

"They would have to take the entire cosmos as a referent, which cannot be done with assumptions that exclude anything. The assignment of cause and effect is not balanced and leaves no room and no incentive for the improvement of one's perception." I elaborated.

"I am glad you realize this, my brother," Osawagu smiled broadly.

– Conversations With Osawagu

The Meanings of Words

My father was a schoolteacher who claimed that a job worth doing should be done well. He also claimed that the best teachers should be teaching at the earliest grade levels, so he taught first grade. Since he believed that one-on-one instruction was best, he was strictly tutorial. Needless to say, he did not teach in a public school. Instead, he taught in a parochial school where he had freedom to excel. He was a potent factor in my development, and I relied on the accuracy and depth of his scholarship.

At age six I happened to ask him, "What does the word *idea* mean?"

"Look it up in the dictionary," was his laconic response.

"Aw, papa! You could just tell me. Why do I have to look it up?"

"You are not going to get very far if you rely on what people tell you. You have to look up words for yourself and study them, or you won't know what is going on."

He had me get the unabridged dictionary, and I got an on-the-spot lesson in its use. I was not keen on it at the time, but I benefited and have remembered it ever since. It was an important early lesson.

Newspeak

In his prophetic and insightful book, 1984, George Orwell describes the enslavement of the human race. One of the key mechanisms was the development of a jargon called newspeak. By using words contradictorily, newspeak defined most of the meaning out of the language it replaced. This made thinking and communication difficult.

Not that people think in words. Rather, they think in ideas, pictures and concepts. But, words are the codes or address system for groupings of mental images. By way of words thoughts are evoked.

If a word is clearly defined, the mental images associated with it are rich and cogent. Then thinking is fruitful and exciting. Conversely, if the meanings of words are blurred, the mental images associated with them are obscured. Then we become faceless, grey men with little more to look forward to than bread and circuses.

What Goes?

For most of my school years my father sent me to a public school. He seemed to think it would give me insight. I do not know what he thought about the academic standards, but he may not have thought too well of them as he often would quiz me about what I was learning in school. In any event, it was not until eighth grade, under the tutelage of a hard-bitten relic of an English teacher, that I encountered serious instruction on using the dictionary. This old woman taught us to use the biggest dictionary we could lay hands on, preferably an unabridged, and to use it for everything, even the simplest words like *a, and, for, but,* and *the.*

How many school children can bounce right back at you a clear definition of one of these simple words when asked? Sure, I know they can spell them. They use them all the time. But how many can define them fast enough and well enough to be reading them at the rate of three or four hundred words a minute?

Is it any wonder, then, that I can give a neighbor a copy of *Acres, U.S.A.,* ask how he liked it, and receive a response like, "I tried to read that thing, but it didn't make much sense." I believe this means he put it down, popped another brew, microwaved his TV dinner, and watched a ball game on the tube instead. If one cannot think when challenged to, it is disquieting. Then the comfort of bread and circuses is necessary.

Words of great importance have lost their meaning for most of the population. Such is the word *science.* Science is the true belief system of modern times. The man-on-the-street believes science has an explanation for everything. In order to hedge his bets, he may go to church. But his true belief, his restraining dogmas, his hope for salvation in the here and now, comes down to science. One need only look at where he turns when ill to see. The pain and fear of injury and disease strips him of his hypocrisies.

Defining Science

Even though science is the *de facto* religion of today's masses, what does the word *science* mean? Those claiming to be scientists usually say it is not a religion. They assert there is no proof of reality beyond the senses, as if thoughts, desires, goals, determination, and imagination do not exist.

I believe more than half of the meaning has been defined out of the word *science.* My *Webster's Second International Unabridged* gives as the primary definition of science: "1.(a) (archaic) Possession of knowledge, as contrasted with ignorance or misunderstanding; as,. *science* in nature's mysteries. (b) Knowledge possessed as a result of study and practice."

Are we not to wonder when the primary definition of a word has become archaic? Why should it be so? And neither definition says anything about science being divorced from religion or having to deal exclusively with the senses.

The Deficient Definition

In school I was taught a definition which said science was a systematic study and classification of facts leading to the establishment and verification of general laws, chiefly by induction and hypothesis. Most people think of this as *the* definition of science, but in reality it is the fourth definition in my unabridged. With its restrictive limits, this minor definition is taught as the only definition. This typifies the self-serving propaganda of elitists who set themselves up as priests, pretending that hypotheses, theories, laws, and axioms are the heart and soul of science. Forget observation and practice, and substitute specialized study and experiment. Is it any wonder people are blind to anything outside the limits of their postulates? This is empire building by confiscating the definition of words, and we should examine its results.

Results of Newspeak

I came from a home where alternative ideas and explanations were exchanged.

At school, however, I was taught that science was based on the delineation of fundamental principles, although I was not taught what these fundamental principles were in any comprehensive fashion. In short, I was taught to have faith in higher authority and not be too critical. Was this the general trend?

I believe this set the stage for the science "professors" to insinuate that the ordinary Joe Doakes is better off not attempting scientific investigations on his own. Instead he should leave things to the experts. They will tell him what to believe. If Joe wants to get by, he should reject anything not endorsed by the experts. The more tightly closed Joe's mind is, they suggest, the safer he is.

Following this line of thinking, a farmer need only do as the experts recommend, and he will be safe.

Actually, this is just when farmers have been the most gullible, and subjected to the greatest physical, mental, emotional and spiritual hazards.

The Meanings of Words   83

There is an archaic Anglo-Saxon word: *"Fode--to beguile, fool; to lull to a delusion of security."* Is it because the farmer has lost this word that he has been so successfully beguiled in our time? It used to be farmers were amongst the hardest people to put something over on. But, without a meaningful language, farmers too can be misled.

Chapter VIII

When I launched my farming career I talked to the county agent, the experiment station scientists, the salesmen at the Coop and neighboring farmers for information and ideas. Also I figured Rodale Press was a likely resource. Nevertheless, I soon found these inadequate. Even after Peter Escher set me on the right track it took me eight years to gain enough knowledge and skill that I could farm, and another four years before I was farming successfully. Furthermore, I knew of no schools that taught what I needed to know.

Did everyone have to take such an arduous road? Would it work? I saw a number of people move to the country and try to farm, only to become discouraged and return to the city.

From the very beginning my reason for farming was to meet needs, and one of the sorest needs was for research and training. I joined a couple dozen other biodynamic farms nationwide in conducting research and offering apprenticeships.

Such a program is for those who are serious about learning. Dilettantes may as well be discouraged. I usually ask for a minimum commitment of one year, though two or three years might better prepare people for starting out successfully on their own.

As far as I know, all biodynamic farms that offer training provide room and board in exchange for labor and instruction. Though they may offer a spending money allowance (stipend) I doubt thatmany offer apprentices wages. A listing of farms offering training can be obtained from the BD Association. (See Appendix I.)

Of course, everyone is an individual and learns in his own way. Some are already working the land and need only see some examples and get a little guidance. Others need closer supervision as well as hands-on experience. Some can probably sort things out from reading and experimenting on their own. Of course, as more families farm biodynamically, people will grow up learning how.

"If you think that your belief is based upon reason, you will support it by argument, rather than persecution, and will abandon it if the argument goes against you. But if your belief is based on faith, you will realize that argument is useless, and will therefore resort to force either in the form of persecution or by stunting and distorting the minds of the young in what is called 'education'."

— Bertrand Russell

Biodynamic Training

As yet, biodynamic agriculture has few adherents. Often people hear about it, investigate superficially, and write it off. Why?

It requires few outside inputs. It passes the tests of being a regenerative system that reliably produces foods of high quality, and it is economically viable. Why, then, is it passed over and ignored? Is this an example of the fear of success?

A New Way of Thinking

Biodynamic agriculture, rather than theorizing, proceeds from what is known. It is known that there is a plant kingdom and an animal kingdom. Their functions are different and complementary. Plants are formative. They build. Animals are transformative, and they recycle or break down and rebuild.

Conventional scientists are apt to say, "Plants build through photosynthesis."

This is all right since plants do photosynthesize. But the BD practitioner is likely to take exception to the implication that photosynthesis is all that is involved in the plant's building. Far from being all, it is only one of the many features of how plants build. It is sloppy thinking to suggest otherwise.

Again, the conventional investigator may say the animal breaks down plant tissues with digestive enzymes. No doubt he will acknowledge that in most cases there is a certain amount of chewing involved. But, the BD practitioner can only shake his head since he knows animal digestion and nervous development run parallel, and both these activities are transformative. For one thing, how does the animal select what it chooses to eat?

Digestive enzymes are not all that count, and knowledge of such details does not explain everything. The biodynamic investigator knows that, overall, animals have a digestive impulse. Enzymes play a part in this digestive impulse, but there is a lot more. Much of the detail is yet undiscovered.

The biodynamic investigator does not pretend to know every detail. He looks at the broader picture and talks of the formative or digestive impulses as a whole. He concentrates on the process of observing the functioning of this digestive impulse so that he learns more and more about it. He avoids jumping to (incomplete) conclusions.

Biodynamic practitioners are likely to talk about formative forces, digestive impulses, cosmic and earthly influences as generalities that they know exist in the broader scheme of things. Though they may know numerous details, they do not want to lose sight of the larger picture. It is better to refrain from citing details as though these are all that exist. This puzzles and annoys people who are so immersed in details that they form snap conclusions, incomplete theories and mistaken assumptions.

Mathematical Proof

Particularly since Immanuel Kant there has been widespread acceptance that science must rest on a mathematical foundation. I like mathematics as much as anyone, but I must point out that mathematics rests on unproven statements called axioms. For example, mathematics assumes that equalities exist. This often is a convenient assumption, but it also is absurd. Nowhere in nature are any two things the same. Before two things can be treated as equal, one must disregard subtle differences as inconsequential.

As a biodynamic practitioner I know that planting corn today is not the same as planting corn tomorrow or the next day. What all the differences are, I do not know. But I am not so confused as to think that there are none. This unflinching scientific accuracy sets a biodynamic practitioner apart as a little odd. It also is a key to success.

Some inquirers may be turned off when they cannot take a course complete with textbook, classroom, instructor, and test papers, thereafter calling themselves biodynamic experts. That is okay. Biodynamic expertise is not a theoretical study. It grows out of first-hand experience.

To Educe

The biodynamic tutor must give individual attention to the apprentice, as expertise is educed, or drawn out. Biodynamic agriculture is concerned with the known, which is concealed by misconceptions, assumptions and automatic behavior. Tutors must bring these occlusions to the fore with their guidance and questioning, and students must endeavor to see those things that get in their way. By directing the attention of the apprentice with questions, instructions and activities, the tutor may get an apprentice to understand the nature of his stumbling blocks. This is the essence of study. Memorization and recital are superficial or even counter-productive by comparison.

For example, when I began farming I assumed that it was necessary to add only organic matter to revive barren land. This meant hauling large quantities of organic materials to the farm. Problems arose, as this went beyond what I could be certain of. In fact, had I paid closer attention I would have known better.

I got my organic materials from mills and animal confinement operations where these wastes were toxic problems. I should not have assumed that large quantities of these things would make my land thrive when plainly their sources were toxic waste sites. But until my activity rubbed my nose in my preconceived ideas I could not progress in understanding. I did not need so much organic matter. I only needed to handle it rightly.

So, to a certain extent apprentices must be allowed to err so that the causes of error are elucidated.

Optimum Balances

There are, of course, some general guidelines. The rapid reclamation of worn-out land depends on achieving an optimum dynamic balance between plant and animal impulses. This means maximizing both active leaf surface and digestive activity.

Collecting leaves from city streets or bagasse from a mill simply brings in substances. Depending on how they are used, these substances may or may not be of much benefit. Trucking them in leaves the fuller activities of these plants behind.

Nor is it enough simply to truck in manure. One really needs the animals themselves to obtain the dynamics required for self-sufficient agriculture. Even then, just having diverse kinds of plants and animals on the farm does not mean they are functioning in an optimum relationship or at an optimum level.

Many plants, on reaching the flowering stage, die back and their leaves cease to function. If this dead vegetation is left in place it thwarts regrowth and wastes potential. Thus cutting hayfields at the blossoming stage makes better use of plant potential.

Likewise if a pasture is continually grazed and the grasses and legumes kept short, they never develop much leaf surface or roots. This means wasting plant potential, and it also wastes animal potential as there is less for the animals to eat. Grazing mixed grass and legume pastures one day per month has the added benefit of stimulating the nitrogen fixing legumes, which tend to bloom sooner than the grasses. This is a good way to utilize both plant and animal potential to build fertility. If large pastures are divided up into a number of smaller paddocks and grazed in rotation, much more is made out of both plants and animals.

Corn, pumpkins and soybeans are diverse and robust summer annuals which can be grown together on the same plots. Rye, vetch, turnips and rape are similarly robust winter combinations. Likewise bees, chickens, cows, pigs and earthworms are productive farm animals which can share a common environment. The possible combinations are numerous.

In my market vegetable plots I have forty inch wide beds with thirty inch wide mowable permanent coverstrips in between. This conserves soil and allows good access even in wet weather. It also allows for fifty or more plant and animal species to thrive symbiotically in the same location. I have a rear-bagging lawnmower and can feed the mower clippings to my chickens. Moreover, mowing my paths is much easier than cultivating them.

By working at the day-to-day activities of the farm, the apprentice has the opportunity to get an understanding of how optimum dynamic balances may be achieved and maintained.

General Guidelines

When a plant finishes its growth and dies, its protoplasm tends to leach and be taken up by other organisms. However, much is locked up in the fibrous tissues left behind. Without the digestive activities of animals, plant fibers would be much slower to break down and return to the soil. Thus a diversity of both plant and animal species is needed to assure rapid recycling of plant materials, as successful biodynamic farms show.

As the above suggests, farm animals are valuable above all for their manure. Treating manure as a disposal problem wastes animal potential. On a biodynamic farm, manure production is of great importance. Composting and enhancing manures with the BD preps brings digestive impulses to their highest expression. All in all, biodynamic agriculture goes far beyond simply growing foods without chemicals. It establishes a resilient, self-sufficient, farm organism that produces wholesome foods which are supportive of both mind and body.

These foods are important, not only for those suffering from illness, but for those who wish to function at a higher level. Above all, they do the most good for children who are not yet fully developed, and the sooner in life they get this kind of nourishment the more good it does.

Chapter IX

The next three chapters on making and using the BD preps are the heart of biodynamic agriculture. Biodynamic agriculture goes beyond simply being a wholesome, self-sufficient, biologically diverse system of farming. Its intent is to provide nourishment for the whole human being. This means not only providing substance, but also nourishment in terms of life, motivation and personality. In other words, food should not only nourish us physically, but also etherically, astrally and egoically.

With the exception of Steiner's Agriculture, *all the presentations of biodynamic agriculture I have seen, whether they have stemmed from the Biodynamic Associations or whether they have come from biodynamic proponents such as Alan Chadwick and John Jeavons, down play or make no mention of the biodynamic preparations. Whether this is squeamishness, a desire to keep key knowledge secret, a failure to fully understand the importance of these preparations or a wish to avoid going beyond the bounds of what is accepted by conventional academicians hardly matters. One of the chief reasons for this book is that these things must be laid on the line.*

I have heard it argued that people are not ready for this material, and when Rudolf Steiner presented it in his agriculture course he did so to people prepared in advance to understand. To a certain extent this is true.

At this point, of course, anyone can buy a copy of Agriculture *and study what Steiner's indications were. Unfortunately reading words like* astral *and* etheric *and grasping their intended meanings are two different things. Steiner's indications came from the viewpoint of spiritual science. How many are prepared for that?*

For the most part people take as their starting point what they learned in school--conventional science. Conventional science contends that all we can prove is the physical facts, and the easiest way to be taken for a goofball is to start talking about a spiritual world with etheric, astral, and egoic components.

While many realize there is more to being human than just the physical flesh, there is, on the other hand, justifiable skepticism. It is good to be wary of shysters who would prey on credibility and waste our time, money and efforts on unproductive fantasies.

Of course, it is always revealing to see where the money goes. One of the most encouraging of all signs is the fact that with biodynamic agriculture nobody is making money from selling the method. In fact, most of those who have succeeded in spreading biodynamic agriculture, such as Peter Escher, Harvey Lisle and particularly Alex Podolinsky, have donated their time and efforts to those they believed committed to following through with this work.

One example of this dedication, Josephine Porter made BD preps available for decades to Americans unable to make their own. She charged, if anything, insufficiently to cover costs. After her death Hugh Courtney took on her work and expanded it, with capital investment from the Biodynamic Association. It is my understanding that Alex Podolinsky does much the same thing in Australia and produces large quantities of preps at very low cost. But nothing could give greater security and lower cost than farmers making their own, which is one of the purposes of committing these methods to print.

As to whether people are prepared for this information or not, we will see. For my own part nothing makes me more impatient and distrustful than mystifying how a method works. The value of these procedures can best be tested by putting them into practice.

"Is it then so great a secret, what God and mankind and the world are? No! But none like to hear it, so it rests concealed."

-Goethe

About 500 and 501

In 1924, when Rudolf Steiner introduced the homeopathic agricultural medicines now called the biodynamic preparations, he indicated that "The most important thing is to make the benefits of our agricultural preparations available to the largest possible areas over the entire earth, so that the earth may be healed and the nutritive quality of its produce improved in every respect."

Yet, so far the techniques of making and applying these preparations can hardly be said to be public knowledge, and the preparations have been applied to only a small portion of the earth.

Even though biodynamic agriculture has been around a long time, few know much about it. Partly this is because it is not easy to grasp. BD agriculture is holistic and seeks to take into account all that is. This is an unaccustomed approach. It does not derive from a piecemeal study of soils, crops, insects, breeding, etc. as our schools teach, but rather it puts these all together in a broad picture that includes the farmer, his customers, his resources, labors, hopes and ideals. For truly, without all these coming together, we would not have agriculture.

For starters, holistic thinking acknowledges the existence of both physical and spiritual reality. Thus it follows that there not only is, physically, the farmer, but he must also have intelligence, feeling and determination. In short the farmer must be spiritually real, with the spiritual reality permeating the physical reality. How does it do so?

The physical body is primarily made up of carbon, hydrogen, oxygen, nitrogen and a little sulphur. Associated with these substances are various elements of ash or clay, of which lime and silica are the earthly and cosmic opposites. Carbon provides the basis for form and individuality, oxygen for life and vitality, nitrogen for sensation and desire, sulphur for initiating activity and hydrogen the bridge that allows things to coalesce on the one hand and disperse on the other. Just as the various combinations of these physical elements give rise to the physical body, so too the spiritual components combine to produce consciousness, emotion and will for the human being.

Aberrating physical processes cannot help but aberrate spiritual processes. For instance, agricultural overuse of nitrogen in its crudest, most reactive forms has resulted in a society bent on instant, unsophisticated gratification in the sense and desire (astral) realm. And, as our soils become more and more deprived of oxygen and plants increasingly are led to depend on soluble fertilizers instead of solid soil, the life (etheric) force of our food supply declines and there is decreasing vitality and increasing illness. Moreover, as humus levels decline plants have less carbon in the soil environment to provide them with formative force so that people increasingly have poorly developed egos and insufficient ability to stick up for themselves. Modern agricultural practices have even resulted in mineral deficiencies in food so that physically people lack in substance. Bringing carbon, hydrogen, oxygen, nitrogen and sulphur, along with the necessary mineral elements, into refined, balanced and harmonious relationships on our farms will result in food that nourishes us better both physically and spiritually, and a society that reflects this.

The biodynamic preparations are designed to address these problems, and there is nothing really difficult about making the preps. All are from naturally occurring materials. If one or another ingredients cannot be found in a given locality, they may be obtained nearby or suitable substitutes found. Because biodynamic preparations are homeopathic medicines, only small quantities need be used for the treatment of large areas. With a little patience, determination and effort enough preps of good quality could be made to treat the entire earth.

Making BD 500

BD 500 is made from the manure of mature cattle, with good digestive activity. If they are a horned breed it is probably preferable that they have their natural horns. This manure is packed into cow horns, if possible those from the surrounding district. It is important that the horns be as thick and heavy, or have as high a weight to volume ratio, as possible. In general cows have much thicker, heavier horns than bulls or steers, and they produce superior results.

Since cattle have such a thorough digestive activity their manure and horns are usually preferred. Leeway exists, however. For instance, hooves could be used in the place of horns if no horns were available. Again the higher the weight to volume ratio the better. Sheep or horse manure could be used if the farm had these animals but no cattle, and again the hooves would be suitable, or in the case of the horse, the hair from the mane could be used to wrap the manure up in.

The horns should be packed and buried in the fall, at least a month or so prior to the winter solstice. Ideally this means November in the northern hemisphere and May in the southern. They should be left buried through the entire winter season and on until past Easter--perhaps Pentecost. My experience is that if they are left much longer the surrounding vegetation grows enough that its roots invade the horn pit, feasting on the 500. This may be good for the vegetation, but not for the 500. I like to dig up my horns, clean them off, knock the 500 out into a bucket, screen it and store it in a crock in my cellar.

It is best to bury the horns in rich, deep soil. Humusy soils or clay loams are best, and clay is all right. Sand should be avoided as much as possible. Near the equator the optimum depth of burial may be a little less than the higher latitudes--perhaps 10 or 12 inches. In Canada or northern Europe a couple feet deep might be preferable. Some believe it is better to get below the frost line, which in high

Colorado, for instance, might be pretty deep. In any event the horns should be placed within the fertile layer if at all possible. Personally I feel the frost can do no harm and is even likely to help, so I would put more emphasis on staying within the fertile soil region. Of course, here in north Georgia the frost rarely gets even a foot deep.

There are all sorts of ideas about what are the best locations and ways of placing the horns in the ground. Some like to find junctions of energy lines or construct stone circles at the burial point. Or they may bury their 500 where they already have such a stone circle (sometimes called an energy wheel). Some think the horn should be oriented so that the tip points toward the heavens, and, of course, the horns may be arranged in a vortex, a rosette or whatever is the preference. I imagine that I am attaching the horns to the earth so that the earth's formative forces flow into them in similar fashion to the way these forces flowed into the horns when they were attached to the cows. The excess soil from the burial pit can be mounded up somewhat like a raised bed to encourage the air with its oxygen (etheric forces) and nitrogen (astral forces) to better permeate the burial pit.

No one has made more BD 500 than Alex Podolinsky, who seems to think that much of the above is irrelevant and that what is important is to bury as many horns as possible at one time and place.

As a practical matter I know that when a horn is placed in such a way that it catches and holds water, a nasty, smelly mess results. Since the idea is to use the horn to focus the astral, etheric and formative forces associated with nitrogen and oxygen and carbon upon the manure content, waterlogging can hardly help. Ideally a nitrogen rich, well-oxidized, humusy material should be obtained. This probably means that if the 500 does not come out of the horn black, crumbly and low in odor it should rapidly become that way upon contact with air.

I would have to say there are subtle factors involved in making good BD 500, and that time and experience will help to reveal what is best. The first step is making it in a sensible, even artful--as well as economical--way. Over time various results will be obtained and a sense for what works best will develop.

My personal experience is that the first time a horn is used in making 500 it should produce good results. Empty horns may be stored in the barn at head level with the cows over the summer to recover strength. If anything they may improve on the next use, but, after several burials they become too thin-walled to make good 500. Experiments with storing the horns in a cellar over the summer with the 500 left inside and reburying them for a second or third winter indicate this is a way of making an enhanced preparation. There have been experiments also with potentizing the manure by triturating, or working it intensively, for an hour or so before packing it into the horns. If ordering preps from BD Preps (Courtney), this material has been designated BD X500 and requires only 20 minutes stirring instead of an hour.

What Is BD 500?

Each BD prep relates to specific aspects of nature as exemplified by chemical elements, compounds and their reactions, members of the solar system and certain organs, organisms, organic structures and their activities. Most of all BD 500 relates to carbon in its organic forms, supported by calcium and silica and permeated as much as possible with oxygen and nitrogen so that a rich humus is formed. It is the quintessential humus, which relates to the central nervous system, particularly the brain. Thus, in making 500 we are producing the brain for our farm organism, the basis for intelligence and self-awareness.

Using BD 500

There are probably as many ways of using this prep as there are people to think them up. The standard and most common way is to add a quarter cup of it to 3 gallons of water, stir it very intensively and sprinkle it on an acre of soil.

The water should be of good quality, and Steiner suggested that perhaps it should even be warmed slightly. I am not so sure about warming it, as it is my understanding that water absorbs the most oxygen (and thus the most life force) if it is cold. I do know that polluted river water or chlorinated city water are best avoided.

A rule of thumb in America is to use a handful, roughly a quarter cup (60 cc.) or one and a quarter ounces (40 grams) weight to three gallons (11.5 liters) of water for application to one acre (0.4 hectares). No two continents are the same. It is my understanding that in Europe a little more 500 is used per unit area. Regardless, this is only a rule of thumb and may change according to circumstance. For instance, if a small isolated city lot or garden is being sprayed, the same amount of 500 might be applied as ordinarily would cover an entire acre. Conversely if an enormous acreage was being sprayed the actual amount of 500 applied could be reduced by as much as one part in ten or more. The amounts can be determined by dowsing. Commonly in practice, however, there is enough 500 available (especially if one is making it oneself) that even for spraying large acreages no reduction in quantity is needed.

Stirring is a homeopathic potentization procedure and should go as follows. Stir strongly around the edge of the stirring vessel (crock, bucket, barrel or large, cylindrical tank) so that the entire contents are rapidly rotating and a vortex is formed reaching toward the bottom of the container. Then, quickly reverse the direction so that the contents seethe round in the opposite direction and a new vortex is formed. Whereupon the direction is again reversed and the solution goes again through chaos toward a new vortex. This is repeated every twenty seconds to a minute or so for roughly an hour.

Harvey Lisle has suggested that because the 500 shows strong earthly forces and induces pendulums to swing clockwise (in the northern hemisphere) that it might best be potentized by stirring entirely in the clockwise direction in order to more strongly intensify its natural forces. I have tried this and believe I received much benefit where such 500 was sprayed. Yet, I cannot escape the feeling that nitrogen and oxygen, along with their astral and etheric influences, are brought into the spray better during the seething chaos when the stirring is reversed.

As soon as possible after stirring, the 500 should be sprayed on the land. Depending on the quantity mixed and the area to be covered, the 500 can be filtered so as to pass through spraying equipment. After all, it is not the material so much as the forces, which in stirring are transferred to the water, that must go on the field. For small areas it can be sprinkled by hand by dipping a large brush in a bucket and slinging it in wide arcs as one walks briskly along anointing the fields.

500 is best sprayed in the late afternoon or evening, and may be sprayed several times a year on the same land. It is commonly applied in conjunction with cultivation, and often is used in the fall, winter, spring and three weeks or so before any planting. Maria Thun recommends spraying both the 500 and the 501 at least three times apiece for each crop from cultivation and planting to harvest.

For my 14 acre farm and six acre market garden I do not need much in the line of stirring or spraying equipment. Larger farmers such as Fred Kirchenmann, Ken Soda or Bob Steffen have made custom automatic stirring machines and tractor driven spray equipment suitable for spraying hundreds of acres at a time. In Australia where farms tend to be quite large and far more than a million acres are under BD management, stirring machinery is standard equipment. Sometimes several machines and spray rigs are used for a single application.

Making Homeopathic Potencies

Field spraying is not the only way of using 500. It can be made into homeopathic potencies by taking roughly three grams of 500 in nine tenths ounces of water, and potentizing it by succussion (very vigorous shaking or pounding) for three minutes. This makes the basic or "mother" material. Then a tenth of an ounce is added to nine tenths water and potentized again for three minutes for the D1 or 1x potency (D as in decimal or x as in the Roman numeral for ten). For the 2x potency a tenth of an ounce of 1x is added to nine tenths of an ounce of water and potentized, again for three minutes. Each successive potency is made from the one before it in this fashion. The potencies can be taken as high as is wished. Small amounts of potentized 500 can be made like this for use as seed soaks, medicinal treatments for plants and animals, reagents in radionic devices, or whatever. Lily Kolisko's research on which potency yields the best results suggested the 6th and 29th potencies might be best. I dowse for which potency to use in each situation.

I use potencies in my Cosmic Pipe, though not always the same potency. For 500 and barrel compost I commonly use the 6th or 8th potencies and bury them three or four inches deep along the east side of my pipe where the base coil is.

Making BD 501

This preparation is complementary to the BD 500. In making the 500 manure was packed in the cow horn and buried for the winter. With the 501 finely ground (colloidal) silica flour is packed in a cow's horn and buried for the summer. The silica material is moistened into a dough or paste and the horn filled with it. Commonly quartz crystal is used, ground finely in a mortar with an iron pestle and then ground even finer between plates of glass. Steiner indicated that other silicious minerals such as orthoclase or feldspar could be used if need be.

A method for crushing crystals that works quite well is to take a length of steel pipe (2 or 3 feet long and no more than 2 inches in diameter) and weld a heavy steel piece over one end. Then another steel bar (or pipe) of smaller diameter that fits snugly inside is used as a plunger. The inner bar should be very heavy and somewhat longer than the outside pipe. The end either should be flat or have shallow grooves in order to crush effectively. Quartz crystal can be placed inside the outer pipe and the inner plunger lifted and dropped repeatedly until the crystals are pulverized. Further grinding between two plates of heavy glass yields a very fine, white powder such as a chemist might use for making silicic acids.

A very good experimental 501 (designated as 501C, as in crystal) was made, however, from crystals fine enough to pass through a 60 mesh screen, separated out of Arkansas rectorite clay. This material was not ground at all, and contained a high percentage of well-formed, tiny crystals. This goes to show, once again, a certain amount of leeway in how preparations may be made. The effectiveness of this experimental 501C supports the argument that these preparations work primarily because of the forces involved, since before this 501C goes on the field the tiny crystals must be filtered out so they do not clog spray nozzles. The actual spray that goes on the field need not contain much if any material.

It does not seem quite so important here that the soil be deep where the 501 is buried, but it probably should not be placed below the fertile layer. A suitable juncture of energy lines may be found for its burial. Because the 501 has the characteristic of an out vortex, in contrast to the 500, some feel the horn tips, where the horn walls are thickest, should be buried pointing downward. Again I like to think more in terms of attaching the horns to the body of the Earth.

In late autumn the 501 should be dug up and stored. Unlike the 500, which is best kept in a cellar and in the dark, the 501 may be kept in a window sill or other protected but sunny location. There have also been experiments with reburying 501 more than one summer to produce an enhanced material.

What Is BD 501?

Where the BD 500 involved catalyzing good humus formation in the soil and creating the basis for nervous activity, the BD 501 makes the farm sensitive. 501 complements the 500. It attunes the farm to its surroundings. What good is our central nervous system without our senses? The 501 provides the farm with what amounts to our sensory organs, as well as other aspects of sensitiveness.

Using BD 501

After the BD 500 has been applied, the 501 may be sprayed the very next morning. I believe the sooner after the 500 the better as this has a wonderful balancing effect on the land and atmosphere.

For some reason here in North America there has been much wider application of BD 500 than of BD 501. Yet, because of the lush nature of our continent, and especially because of the cloudy, rainy and forested nature of much of the American east, southeast and northwest, 501 can be especially beneficial and should be applied, if anything, more frequently than the 500. Undoubtedly this is much less true in the hot, dry and intensely sunny regions of the midwest and southwest. Not that one preparation should be used to the exclusion of any of the others.

Probably little can be gained by use of the 501 where the 500 has not previously been applied. The two are, of course, both important, and they can hardly be expected to give good results without both being used even if one is used somewhat more frequently than the other.

For a one acre application of 501 only one gram is needed for three gallons of water. Warming the water for the 501 is probably more important than for the 500. At least, Steiner stated it should be warmed. I do not imagine this means heating it to much more than the temperature of the human blood, however, and in the summertime here in Georgia atmospheric temperature is probably good enough.

It is stirred for one hour in the same fashion as the 500. If it is stirred without reversing it should be stirred in the counterclockwise direction because of its peripheral, cosmic forces. After an hour's vigorous stirring the 501 should be applied as soon as possible.

It should always be sprayed in the early morning as compared to the late afternoon for the 500. Where the 500 forces sink into the soil just as the dew falls in the evening, the 501 forces rise as the dew evaporates in the morning. Rather than sprinkling it on in large drops like the 500, it should be applied if possible as a fine mist. Normally it is used as a foliar spray permeating the region of the leaves and the atmospheric space above the plant. It may also be applied to the soil, as in the case of freshly cultivated land following an application of 500. There is even the possibility that it might be beneficial to inject it as much as six or eight inches deep during cultivation, perhaps to dry out tight, wet soil. If applied too close to mid-day, burned foliage may result.

Because it is so effective in stimulating the upward raying forces of silica it is especially beneficial for silica rich grasses and grain crops, such as corn or wheat, which ray forth from the soil. It has a strong power to stimulate fruit and seed formation, and perhaps it might force young trees to bear fruit earlier than is good for them if it is applied too soon in their development or too frequently.

It also has the virtue of improving the flavor and nutritional value of crops, as well as making them more resistant to diseases and insects. Repeated applications should enhance these effects. One of the ways you will know the 501 is working is whether insects and diseases become less of a problem and crops taste better.

As far as homeopathic dilutions go, Lily Kolisko's work indicated that the 5th and the 28th potencies were generally the most effective. If applied with a Cosmic Pipe, 501 should be placed above ground in the well of the pipe, at the junction where the top and bottom pieces join and the coil pickup is. Commonly, however, in my Cosmic Pipe I use the 11th or the 13th potencies according to what my dowsing indicates.

In Summary

Fortunately these preps go beyond the world-view of most of those who might otherwise try to suppress them. Thus they tend to be ridiculed and ignored. Moreover, the low cost and independence of these procedures makes them attractive for farmers.

For the same reasons it is unlikely that professional researchers will investigate them. Paid researchers usually want to increase yields with some industrial product application which has short term potential to make money for the farmer. When it comes to the real point of agriculture--nourishment--very little comes out of such work. What follows is a comment Steiner made in this connection.

"How different it is in all that is here said out of Spiritual Science! Underlying it, as you have seen, is the entire household of Nature. It is always conceived out of the *whole*. Therefore each individual measure is truly applicable to the whole, and so it should be. If you pursue agriculture in this way, the result can be no other than to provide the very best for man and beast. Nay more, as everywhere in Spiritual Science, here too we take our start above all from *man* himself. Man is the foundation of all these researches, and the practical hints we give will all result from this. The end in view is the best possible sustenance of *human* nature. This form of study and research is very different from what is customary nowadays."

Chapter X

A booklet published in 1951 concerning the manufacture and use of the BD preps stated in its preface, "The editors most earnestly hope that this publication will not give rise to discussions of the making, use and effect of the preparations in circles other than those already closely and intimately associated with study and practice of anthroposophical agriculture."

I believe this sort of attitude has given biodynamic agriculture a flavor of having something it is hiding.

The old peasant traditions were lost largely because inner details were kept secret, the proprietary knowledge of a small number of initiates. This was not a strong position. Not only did this make peasant medicine vulnerable to accident and suppression, but when errors and misconceptions arose they were not questioned and affairs went from bad to worse.

One of the best ways to perpetuate dogma and prejudice is to keep these from coming to light as such. In this regard, one of the most refreshing things about modern science is that it publishes and teaches openly to all who wish to learn.

Although the anthroposophical agriculture referred to above grew out of the work of Rudolf Steiner, I have not found anywhere that he advocated secrecy himself. Wisdom is something that needs to be shared, not buried.

Yes, one needs to be an anthroposophist at heart to become a biodynamic practitioner. But this means being a seeker of wisdom, not a follower of dogma. Amongst other things this means keeping an open mind and investigating all things. It means using all talents and abilities and not getting stuck in ruts, no matter how comfortable they may seem.

In the previous chapter I mentioned dowsing and radionics in connection with making and using the BD preps. I have received a certain amount of criticism for this, and the Demeter Association, which certifies biodynamic farms, for a brief time ruled that anyone who used radionics on their farm could not receive Demeter certification. Such things pass, but they show the difficulty of maintaining an open mind.

Nearly all the complaints I hear about dowsing and radionics amount to fears of mechanical occultism. What is occult, or hidden, is the working of the third force, which is associated with the nuclei of atoms.

Physics presently holds that there are four forces: the force of electromagnetism, the force of gravity, and the strong and weak nuclear forces. As pointed out in chapters II, III and the glossary. however, the idea of polarity is poorly understood by conventional science. Color is thought to be due only to light without the interaction of darkness. Gravity is thought of by itself without its opposite polarity of levity. Modern physics will at some point have to correct itself.

In the sense that a force is an essence which compels, there are but three forces, all involving polarity. These are electricity, magnetism and the third (nuclear) force, which works directly upon the nuclei of atoms but is incompletely and incorrectly understood or hidden (occult for the present).

Steiner went further by suggesting it was the destiny of America to develop mechanical occultism; it was Europe's destiny to develop occult medicine and it was Asia's destiny to develop occult eugenics. Certainly such pioneers in radionics and sympathetic vibratory physics as Abrams, Hieronymus and Keely were Americans, while homeopathy and the medical use of radionics have advanced more in Europe than anywhere else. What is going on in Asia in regard to occult eugenics I do not know, but I do know that one of the most outstanding plant breeders of this century was Vavilov, a Russian. Also, central Asia is the greatest genetic well-spring of agricultural species in the world.

Of course, once the third force is explored and becomes common knowledge it will no longer be occult. It is only occult because it is hidden. Nor should the progress of occult science be feared or impeded. In the final analysis truth and wisdom are free. They only await realization. They are not the private property of any person or organization.

Nor should anyone think these forces come into play only once they are discovered. That is absurd. They have long been going on and will long do so. We can use them better the more we understand them. Until we understand more fully we will have to take such things as the BD preps with a minimum of explanation and a generous dose of open-mindedness.

"Just as when there is a lull in the wind a snowdrift piles up, so when there is a lull in truth an organization springs up."

–Thoreau

The Compost Preps

BD 500 and 501 are followed up by six other preparations which provide support for the farm organism. As with 500 and 501, the methods may seem a little strange initially, but they get good results and deserve investigation.

Making BD 502

502 is made by taking the florets of the common, wild white yarrow (*Achillea millefolium*), enclosing them in the bladder of a male elk, deer or moose, and exposing them to the summer cosmic and winter earthly influences.

Lily Kolisko believed it was important to use a fresh stag bladder to make this preparation, and she had an arrangement with a gamekeeper near Stuttgart to get these. However, the month of June may be a difficult time of year to secure such an item in the U.S. Thus, an inflated, dried bladder is what is usually used.

Many deer hunters do not know precisely what the male elk, deer or moose bladder looks like. It is a whitish, membranous sack, usually with urine in it, attached to the penis and situated in the pelvic region. My experience is that deer hunters field dress their kills, stripping out the heart, lungs and entrails, and packing the carcass off to a slaughterhouse to be cut and wrapped. They may leave the bladder in the carcass, since this organ is snugly positioned in the crotch and can be overlooked. If one cannot get bladders directly from hunters, one may be able to find a slaughterhouse that cuts and wraps game for hunters and explain the need for this organ, intact, with enough of the penis attached to allow it to be inflated.

I insert a ballpoint pen, with the filler removed, down the urether duct. Then I blow it up rather like a balloon, tying off the penis with a string and hanging it to dry by my wood heater. I have never ruptured one this way, and since I get them in the fall and early winter when the wood heater is in use, they dry nicely. In the event there is a hole in the bladder and it will not inflate properly I understand it is possible to poke a balloon down the urether duct (using the pen refill) and inflate the balloon inside the bladder. Then when the bladder is slit open to be stuffed the balloon can be removed.

502 is usually prepared in June, and the yarrow is in bloom where I live at that time. This may not be true everywhere, and some may have to use dried flowers. The florets should be cut from the stalks with as little stem as possible. If the flowers are dried, a decoction made from leftover stalks or from extra dried flowers may be used to moisten them. A moist mass of tiny, rice-like florets is packed into the bladder as firmly as possible through a small cut made in it. Then the bladder is sewn up and hung in the sunshine seven or eight feet off the ground for the summer and fall seasons.

My experience is that if the cord tying off the penis is the only thing holding up the bladder, birds or wind may cause damage. Thus it probably is best to make a sock out of cotton cheesecloth or silk pantyhose to suspend the bladder in.

Sometime in the fall, probably October or early November, the 502 should be buried in a well-marked spot so that it passes the winter and spring in the soil's fertile zone, no more than a foot deep. There is no need to bury it deeply, and if it happens to be in the frost zone over the winter so much the better.

It may have to be protected by something, such as the sock it was hung in, to deter earthworms from invading it. I have not had too much trouble in this regard. As long as I am very careful digging it up I do not worry about losing it or getting soil mixed in.

I have found that if I do not soak the bladder a day or two before burying it, it may remain dry inside and not compost much. I take care not to leach too much juice out when I soak it, but I think it should be moist enough to compost somewhat during burial.

By the next July or August when it is unearthed, it should have had a full year's cycle (and a little extra) of exposure to the cosmic and earthly influences. In this way it spans the polarities of earth and cosmos.

For storage 502 may be kept in a glass container or ceramic crock, surrounded by peat moss, in root cellar conditions. I have built a wooden box filled with peat to hold my compost preps. That makes carrying them convenient. If one is simply ordering preps they may be ordered as needed. If plans for building a storage box are desired they can be obtained from BD Preps in Woolwine. (See appendix.)

What Is BD 502?

It is related to the kidneys and bladder, the function of purification and excretion, and the planet Venus. It improves the farm organism's excretion and purification. Just as the stag is one of the most graceful and sensitive of animals, the yarrow is one of the most beautifully refined and aromatic of plants. Although all the herbs used for the compost preps have a good connection with sulphur, (as seen in their well-cut and deeply lobed leaves) yarrow has a truly exemplary relationship with this key element. It also has a good relationship with potassium, as shown by its strong stalks. Thus it helps the spirit, through the agency of sulfur, to bring potassium into the organic processes of the farm.

Also my radionic experiments show 502 to be one of the best BD preps for detoxifying the soil.

Making BD 503

503 is made from the blossoms of the German chamomile (*Matricaria chamomilla*) enclosed in the small intestines of a bovine and buried no more than a foot deep in fertile soil for the entire winter season.

Here again a local slaughterhouse may be able to supply fresh, good quality, unwashed bovine intestines. If one has cattle taken to slaughter it is possible to get a tremendous amount of small intestines from one animal.

I have found it difficult in my locality to obtain fresh chamomile flowers in October when this prep should be made, so I used dried flowers. A tea can be made from a portion of the flowers to moisten the mass, which is packed into the intestines the same way one would make sausages. These are then buried, no more than a foot deep, in rich soil.

Steiner recommended an especially humus rich place be found where the snow accumulates despite catching good sun. I have been burying my 503 on the south side of the house where the snow slides off the roof. In Georgia, however, we do not always get snow.

In order to grow chamomile I use tea bags for seed, planting the fine material in rows on well-prepared ground. I can plant from April through August, though I find that in the middle of summer I do not have time for weeding. I have (once) been successful in using buckwheat as a nurse crop, cutting it for fodder in the fourth week and letting the chamomile take over. I pretty much just leave the seed on the soil surface, pressing it down and watering if there is no rain.

I like to pick chamomile on flower days (when the Moon is in an air constellation) and dry the flowers on screens in my attic. Picking individual blossoms is exhausting. With a pocket comb, however, I can comb the plant, picking several blossoms at a time and going fairly rapidly. The comb picks six to ten flowers at a pass, and I pinch off the stems on the other side of the comb. I also have used chamomile flowers sold in bulk for herbal medicine, but these are never as good a quality as what I grow.

Along about Easter or Pentecost this prep should be dug up and stored in the cellar in glass or crockery surrounded by peat moss, as with the 502. If properly made this will be the most well-composted prep. I understand that in Steiner's notes for this lecture there was mention of hanging the 503 in the summer sun similar to 502, but this did not become part of the lecture as he delivered it. It may, however, be experimented with. Again, I would suggest that before burial the sausages should be soaked to moisten them, as I do with the 502.

What Is BD 503?

It is related to the intestines, the functions of digestion and assimilation, and the planet Mercury. It gives the farm organism what it needs for digestion and assimilation. It too relates to sulphur and potassium, but along with them it brings a significant amount of calcium into the picture. Thus, it has the strong attractive or craving power of calcium that pulls nitrogen into the soil. Just as the intestinal wall exerts transformative power on the chyme as it passes over into the blood, the 503 transforms the exhausted organic forms in the soil into nourishment for plants. It also protects from the uptake of toxic compounds, keeping the nutrient fluids pure and well-balanced. Through the calcium, it stabilizes nitrogen in manures, kindling a well-nourished astrality for the farm organism.

Making BD 504

504 is made from the leaves and stems of the stinging nettle (*Urtica dioica*). They are not packed into any animal membrane as they have a sufficient astrality already. They are simply compacted

as a mass and buried in the summertime 10 or 12 inches deep in a pit lined with peat moss, and left for somewhat over a year.

Steiner indicated that this herb, more than any other, might be difficult to find a proper substitute for. It is quite high in both protein and iron. Earthworms love it and will go out of their way to consume it. The only way I have ever gotten any finished 504 was to staple up envelopes of nylon screen about the size of a small throw pillow and stuff these tightly with the herb.

Ordinarily I cut fresh nettles with a scythe and pick them up with a pitchfork, spreading them on screens in my attic until they are dry enough to handle without stinging. Then I crush this up and pack my pillows. These I bury with peat moss on all sides in my 504 pit.

Harvey Lisle wrote an article once about how 504 was the easiest of all the BD preps to make. Maybe for him. But, for me it was the most frustrating until I hit on the method of enclosing it in screen to keep the earthworms out.

In late summer when this prep is unearthed it may be sifted and kept in similar fashion to the 502 and 503.

Stinging nettle loves nitrogenous soils. It grows well on the edges of fields and woods, in amongst the leaves and small, dead branches. Its tender tips are considered a delicacy in many parts of Europe, though they are harvested with gloves and steamed or boiled before eating. However, stinging nettle does not like to grow from seed all that well. It is more easily propagated from underground runners. If you cannot find this plant anywhere in your vicinity you could send me something to cover postage and handling for a few runners. If given a little compost and some light mulch they should grow rapidly.

What Is BD 504?

It is related to the heart and circulation, the energizing process and the Sun. It helps the farm's circulation, giving it heart and energy. Some biodynamic farmers relate it to the planet Mars, but I agree with Maria Thun and Harvey Lisle that it is related to the Sun.

My sense of this prep is that where it comes to the land, even wherever the nettles grow, there is a very warm appearance to the soil. 504 helps both deficiencies and toxicities of iron, energizing related minerals and activating enzymes. 504 is one of the best preps to open up heavy clays and build humus, preparing the soil for nitrogen fixation. It improves the soil's porosity, unlocks micronutrients and protects against anemia.

Making BD 505

In America 505 is usually made from the finely ground outer bark of the white oak tree (*Quercus alba*), which is packed in the cranial cavity of a domestic farm animal's skull and buried for the autumn and winter in a spot where water trickles constantly. In Europe the bark of the English oak (*Quercus robor*) is used, but the English oak is not native in the western hemisphere.

I bury mine around September or October in a little spring which runs a brisk trickle all winter, and is up a wooded hollow along my creek. I have to place a large rock on top. Otherwise dogs home in on it and drag it away. For some reason this prep attracts them strongly. Another method is to cover the 505 with wire mesh fencing and stake it down.

The bark should be from a healthy tree, not a dying tree or one that has been cut down and left to decay. I use my hand-crank Corona mill for grinding up the bark. As to the animal skull, a fresh skull is generally preferable. At one time I used to put my fresh skulls in the compost pile so the earthworms could eat some of the flesh off of them, but perhaps it is better not to do this. No doubt a skull that has kicked around in the sun for a few years is of little value. It may not be a good idea to use skulls for 505 more than once unless there is no alternative.

Lily Kolisko ran tests on various farm animal skulls and found sheep skulls to be excellent, cow skulls were quite good, and pig skulls were more or less satisfactory. I have used mostly cow skulls, but also sheep, goat and pig skulls. I once used a dog's skull, but for some reason I got a poor transformation of the bark and obnoxious odors in the finished material. I threw it out. I have had it suggested to me that only the skulls of herbivorous animals are desirable for 505.

In the spring the 505 may be removed from its soaking place and the (now much darker) bark removed and stored in the cellar packed in peat moss as with the preceding three preps.

To explore the range of possibilities, I made 505 with a previously used goat skull and dried oak bark from a lightning struck red oak (*Quercus rubra*) tree. According to native American lore, the bark from an oak tree struck by lightning has quite special properties. The result looked and smelled very good. Harvey Lisle ran paper disc chromatogram and sensitive crystallization plate tests on it. We also dowsed for its radius of effectiveness when applied to a fruit tree and measured its general vitality with a Hieronymus radionic analyzer. By all tests it was a high quality preparation, though it showed signs of some unique properties. I believe more such experimentation is needed. We cannot simply establish one convention as the only right way.

What Is BD 505?

It relates to the skeleton, the skin, the head and the force of personality, as well as the Moon. It might seem intuitively obvious that, with its high calcium content, 505 establishes the skeletal framework for the farm organism. And, in a certain sense it does. But it goes much further than that. It firmly fixes the egoic force, the individuality of the farm, giving it inner strength, but also outward form. It provides what is necessary for plants to be upright and well-formed, and it develops the farm's immune system, conferring disease resistance on crops.

505 is made up of the outermost skin of a highly evolved plant and the cranial housing for the innermost activities of a highly evolved animal. It includes both the outermost and innermost formative/transformative forces, the skin and brains, so to speak, of the farm organism.

Making BD 506

506 is made from the young blossoms of the common dandelion (*Taraxacum officinale*) enclosed in the mesentery (part of the peritoneum) of a bovine, and buried no more than a foot deep in fertile soil from roughly October or early November until some time around Easter. I am unable on my farm to find enough fresh dandelions in October to be of use, so I pick dandelions in the spring when they are bursting into bloom and are plentiful. I dry them in my attic and save them until fall. Hugh Courtney indicates he prefers dandelions in the early bloom stage when some of the innermost petals are still tightly closed, and if possible he wants them picked on flower days when the moon is in an air constellation. In order to beat the bees to the blossoms it is best to pick as soon as the dandelions open up in the morning.

As for the mesentery, here again it may be necessary to do your own slaughtering or establish a good relationship with a local slaughterhouse. The mesentery is not the entire peritoneum, but is the part that supports the small intestine. Generally it can be cut and sewn into little pillows. Once the pillows are made they are stuffed with moistened dandelion flowers, sewn closed and buried.

In the spring when the 506 is dug up it should be stored along with or in similar fashion to the other compost preps. Except for the 503, it may be the best digested, blackest and stickiest of the six compost preps.

What Is BD 506?

The 506 relates to the liver and the endocrine glands, the developing, regulating, balancing and harmonizing functions, associated with the planet Jupiter. It establishes the proper relationship between potassium and silica and it helps to develop attraction, fullness and health. It helps crops to draw their nourishment from their broader environment, and overcomes obstructions to the flows of forces in the farm's surroundings.

Dandelion, it might be noted, traditionally is used in rainmaking ceremonies to overcome stagnant atmospheric conditions. Also, as far as I can tell, wherever dandelion grows abundantly alfalfa can be planted successfully, and alfalfa is notoriously finicky about growing in the face of interference.

Making BD 507

507 is made by grinding the fresh florets of the valerian plant (*Valeriana officinalis*) to a pulp, placing the pulp on a clean, strong cotton handkerchief, gathering up the edges, and twisting them so as to tighten the mass and force the juice out. The mass will have to be kneaded and twisted repeatedly to extract all the liquid. The result is a dark greenish fluid with a cloudy sediment that is best left unfiltered. I understand that on some BD farms there are hydraulic presses for the extraction of valerian juice. What I use to grind up the flowers is my hand-crank (Corona) grist mill.

This is my idea of an easy prep to make, though at first I had trouble getting a valerian patch going. I pick a flower day along in mid spring when the valerian is at the height of its bloom and I cut the flowers. With scissors I trim all the florets off the stems into a bowl and run them through the Corona mill. It really crushes them up into a paste, from which I squeeze the juice. In just a couple hours I have fresh 507, which I store in a brown glass Worchestershire sauce bottle on a cellar shelf. Because it is likely to ferment, I leave the top of the bottle slightly loose at first to let off pressure. It is all right if it ferments. It does not need a stabilizer.

What Is BD 507?

507 relates to the body's ability to produce heat, the burning process associated with respiration, and the red blood cells. It activates phosphorus, bringing it into the organic process. Many BD farmers have related 507 to Saturn, but I am convinced it relates to Mars.

507 is a warmth giver and it sometimes is used as a foliar spray to protect against late frosts as long as they are likely to be only a degree or two. I would not use it carelessly, however. If it works too strongly it can make plants expire in the blossoming stage.

Using the Compost Preps

In one way or other all BD farms have livestock and make compost. They may add rock powders such as rock phosphate, lime, basalt or granite, since these earthly factors must be added if they are deficient. They may add chipped tree trimmings, sawmill bark, peat, shredded leaves or hay. They also add the preps.

First of all, the shape of the pile is important. It should be well-rounded, either circular, eggshaped, or elongated as a windrow, but not with huge peaks and valleys. Geometric forms have considerable significance, and well-rounded forms conserve energy.

A compost pile needs air and moisture to permeate it, and it should contain a small percentage of good soil or rock powder such as granite or basalt.

Six holes are poked in the pile. I use an old shovel handle or a heavy iron rod for this. Then in five of the six holes a heaping teaspoon of one or another of the first five compost preps is inserted. Since only the 503 and the 506 are sure to be sticky enough to hold together in a lump, a little manure may be used to mix with the looser preps so they can be dropped down their holes intact. It is better if they are kept in lumps. If they are scattered throughout the pile their forces will be diluted and mixed and may interfere with each other.

Traditionally the 507 is diluted and dynamized before use. Approximately 20 to 25 drops are added to a gallon of water and stirred for 15 or 20 minutes in the same fashion as the 500 and the 501. Roughly half of this liquid may be sprayed on the outside of the pile and the rest poured down the sixth hole.

Placement of the Preps

Does it matter how the holes are placed, and which prep goes in which location? Yes. Two holes should be made in the center of the pile and they should be rather deep, though no more than halfway into the pile. The other four holes (or if 500 is to be included, five holes) should be made near the edge of the pile and spaced around the circumference. They should not be so deep, and cannot be since the pile always slopes toward the edges. The 504 and 505--which are made from leaves and stems, or bark, and represent the Sun and Moon--go in the center holes. Just as the leaves, stems and bark draw energy into the plant and hold it, these two preps draw energy into the pile.

The 502, 503, 506 and 507, which are made from blossoms and represent Venus, Mercury, Jupiter and Mars, go around the circumference. Just as the blossoms release the plant's energy, these four preps release energy at the pile's edges. What they release is caught by the 504 and 505 in the center and drawn into the pile. If you are a dowser, it might be a good idea to dowse for which prep goes in which hole. My experience is that 502 and 507 are pairs that should go opposite each other, and the same with 503 and 506.

There is still one more prep that has not yet been discussed. That is the 508. The 508 is the herb, meadow horsetail (*Equisetum arvense*). It may be used either as dried herb or as a decoction or tea. Normally it is used as a field spray to protect against too rapid and watery growth, as it hardens and strengthens plants. When I use this preparation as a field spray I commonly spray it after spraying the barrel compost, so I discuss these two sprays in the next chapter.

Though there is little agreement amongst biodynamic practitioners at this point, Harvey Lisle was one of the first to suggest the 508 represents Saturn. I realize that many treat the 507 as Saturn and the 504 as Mars, but then, what is the Sun? The 501? No, the 501 represents the cosmic surroundings of which the Sun is only a part, just as the 500 represents the Earth itself.

The first time I really made what I thought was beautiful compost was when, by accident, I treated a pile with 508. I had harvested a truckload of horsetail and dried it in my attic. Once it was processed and stored I swept up all the leavings and threw them on the compost pile, thus treating it with 508. When Harvey told me he thought 508 represented Saturn and belonged on the outside of every compost pile, I thought back to that exceptional batch of compost and realized he was right. Since then I have been scattering a little dried horsetail, or sprinkling a decoction of horsetail (the usual form of 508) over the surface of my compost piles, and this has consistently produced excellent composts.

Since I started using the 508 on my compost piles I have been disinclined to spray the 507 over the pile, and I simply put it down its hole. In fact, I usually do not stir it and potentize it any more, although I realize Steiner suggested doing this in his agriculture course. Instead, I mix about 25 drops with a small lump of manure and drop it down its hole. It seems to ray throughout the pile quite well.

I might suggest, at least for beginners, that they mix the 507 and add it to the pile in the traditional way--half down the hole and half sprinkled over the pile. This does work satisfactorily, is by far the commonest method, and perhaps it will avoid confusion. But, my experience with the biodynamic method is that it is not set in concrete, despite what some of its more rigid proponents seem to think. Certainly in the agriculture lectures Steiner said that his recommendations should be experimented with and the best methods determined. It is good to know that there is experimentation going on which may one day result in better methods.

Last but not least, Harvey Lisle puts the 500 in all his compost piles. He says his dowsing experiments show it belongs in every compost pile. I have not jumped on this method yet, though it is hard to say why. I suspect he is right, but I would like to understand it better. I will say this. Harvey has decades of experience with the old ways of doing these things, yet he experiments. He is not stuck in any ruts, and this is a healthy thing. While beginners may be best off learning the tried and true procedures first, all too many thereafter become hidebound. I hope my readers do not do this, as what is written in this book is not the final word.

Large Piles

It has been a while since I made BD compost on a large farm. Back when I worked on a 100 cow dairy farm I was just switching over to the preps from the Pfeiffer compost starter, which is a bacterial culture that, as I understand it, has 500 and the compost preps in it. At that time we used two tractors, one with a front end loader and the other with a PTO-driven manure spreader on the back. We used one dipper of sawmill bark in the bottom of the spreader with three dippers of dairy manure on top. I sprayed down the material in the spreader with the Pfeiffer starter as it was loaded, and then I drove the tractor down to the end of our compost windrow and backed it up to the end of the pile. When I turned on the PTO, the flails tossed the bark and manure out the back as I inched forward with the tractor. This made beautiful, well-aerated windrows about four feet high and eight feet wide. When I started using preps I divided up the windrows into sections about 20 feet long for each set of preps. We made very good compost this way. I always wished I could mix and toss my own compost piles this nicely.

On an even larger scale there are farming operations that use special composting machinery such as has been designed and marketed by Fletcher Sims, Jr. For some time Fletcher advocated the use of the Pfeiffer compost starter. Then he switched to an inoculant developed by Vaclav Petrik, marketed under the name, CompoStar. I have tried some and found it is a very good product. The composts I have seen made with it and large scale composting machinery have all been of high quality. Like the Pfeiffer starter, it has inherent properties that go beyond the mere microorganisms themselves, but I am unable to say how it is produced or just what it contains.

I believe that the sort of composting machinery Fletcher developed is designed to use a sprayed inoculant, and that if you wanted to use the preps with such machinery you might as well use the Pfeiffer starter, or barring that, put a set of preps every twenty feet or so in the windrows after turning them.

Other Applications

The BD preps may be used to treat specific problems and imbalances. The 508, as we will see in the next chapter, is frequently used to hold back watery growth and prevent disease. The 507 can stimulate blossoming, the 506 can help things fill out, the 505 can build immunity, the 504 can get the energy flowing. The 503 can speed up the release of nutrients from soil organic matter, and the 502 can purify the soil. Another way of looking at special applications would be to take a problem and consider which prep or preps might best be used to give relief.

I have used different preps, usually potentized in water like the 507, or diluted homeopathically as outlined in chapter IX, in treating specific problems with soils, crops, and livestock. But my experiments have not been sufficient that I am ready to give a list of recommendations. I leave to the reader to develop his own insights and ideas.

There is also the potential for using various preps as seed soaks. The indications of the agriculture course are that the time of a seed's sprouting is one of the two best times to influence a plant's genetic expression. The other is at the time of pollination and seed formation. Moreover, Barbara McClintock's Nobel prize winning research with corn suggests that genetic mutations occur much more commonly and are much more benign than previously supposed. I have seen evidence that various plants can be influenced beneficially by homeopathic dilutions of the preps. I wish I had more opportunity for experiment, but the growing of market vegetables keeps me really busy. Perhaps someone else will do this. It is a large field of investigation, and considering how seedstocks have degenerated for many crops, this is important work.

Harvey Lisle feels the pull of his dowsing rods as he nears the crossing of energy lines where he has biodynamic preparations buried. Harvey has a number of stones set in a circle, called an energy wheel, around a central stone marking the point where the energy lines cross.

Chapter XI

This chapter wraps up the manufacture and use of the BD preps. Besides covering BD 508, BD Barrel Compost, and a few other odds and ends, it covers methods of getting rid of undesirable species.

From a farmer's point of view, he may need to eliminate bean beetles or groundhogs or some particularly obnoxious weed. Biodynamic agriculture has its own methods for this. But there is the conundrum of how does one know whether it is really safe and desirable to eliminate a species? What is its function? It may seem obnoxious, but if it thrives where other things struggle, does it not belong in the ecology? Would it not be better to discover the function of the species than to eliminate it and leave some underlying problem unaddressed?

Here in Georgia we have a plant called kudzu. It is a vigorous perennial legume which grows where all else fails. It resists drought, stops erosion, turns the red clay subsoil into rich, brown topsoil, and is one of the best fodders for cattle, horses, sheep, goats, pigs, you name it. It is so vigorous that it climbs tall trees and smothers them. It was imported from Japan in the 1930's to repair the ravages of erosion in the southeast. It is loose now, and people tend to believe it cannot be controlled. Yet, I have never seen it growing in a continuously occupied pasture. The animals graze it so intensively they kill it. To control it one need only fence it in and pasture animals on it. All farm animals eat it. It is in the arrowroot family, and in Japan it is prized even for human consumption, as the highest grade food starch powders are made from its roots.

When a species grows like this, it may be more trouble fighting than it is worth. Better to put it to use. Kudzu can be used to reclaim ruined land, and it could hardly be much cheaper to grow. In many places it is a blessing rather than a curse. It may be hard to cut and cure out as hay, but it could be excellent in a rotational grazing scheme.

A couple of other plant species, common in Georgia, that fall into this same category are water hyacinth and bamboo. Both of these plants grow vigorously, and, if managed properly, can be of great benefit. Water hyacinth was one of the mainstays of Mayan agriculture in Central America. Bamboo is one of the most important plants in the Orient. Yet, at least in Georgia, there are many places they are fought against as though they were amongst man's worst enemies--and maybe in some places they are troublesome. But, we also must ask whether mankind is not its own worst enemy. Misperception and misconception may be the most dangerous hazards we face.

Nevertheless, this chapter includes methods for getting rid of unwanted species. I can suggest these methods be used with discretion. That is a warning. Be careful not to overdo it. I truly believe that people are better off knowing these methods than remaining in ignorance. I can see what murderous weapons automobiles can be, and yet I see that most people are safe drivers.

There have been occasions when this information has been held back in the past. Some have feared the public was not prepared for it. There is a good bit of information in Steiner's agriculture lectures that some have imagined--sort of along the lines of the government classifying so many things secret--was dangerous for the public to know. Regardless, the time has come for openness.

"Man himself, inasmuch as he makes use of his healthy senses, is the greatest and most exact physical apparatus; and it is the greatest evil of modern physics--that one has, as it were, detached the experiment from man and wishes to gain knowledge of nature merely through that which artificial instruments show."

—Goethe

Rounding Out The Picture

Discussion of the biodynamic preparations is not complete without identifying some means for holding in check the watery growth process which is strongest at the full moon. Especially when there is plenty of rain this can run rampant, stretching plant growth too thin. This is the underlying cause of plant diseases. If plants grow too lushly they become weak, and in this condition they are susceptible to rusts, mildews and fungi. BD 508, the horsetail preparation, is the biodynamic farmer's chief medicine for tempering the watery growth forces and ensuring the plant achieves healthy maturity.

Making BD 508

508 is made by boiling up a strong decoction of dried meadow horsetail (*Equisetum arvense*), also called shavegrass or scouring rush. I usually boil up a pound of dried herb to 10 or 12 quarts of water. I simmer the decoction for 20 or 30 minutes at a gentle boil. The result is a concentrated extract that can be diluted one part in ten and potentized for spraying on the fields. It is perhaps best to let it ferment a few days before use. It may also be used for making homeopathic potencies.

Harvey Lisle tells me he prefers not to boil this preparation, but instead, makes it in a large, transparent container as a sun tea. I have tried this, but felt the results were inconclusive and have stuck to my old methods. If I am going to treat 8 to 10 acres by mixing up a 24 to 30 gallon batch in a barrel, I find making 3 to 4 gallons of the decoction and adding this to the larger quantity more convenient.

Probably because Steiner mentions this preparation separately as a means of lessening or holding back the watery growth forces associated with the Moon, 508 has been ignored more than any other preparation. Many BD growers have not used it as one of the preps, but rather as a treatment to avoid fungus problems and to be used only occasionally, if at all. However, it complements the other six compost preparations so well that it belongs with them. Without the 508 the compost preps, especially in high rainfall areas such as the eastern U.S., can encourage rampant growth and crops that fail to conserve their energy so as to reach healthy maturity. For one thing, four out of six of the compost preps are made from flowers, which more than any other plant organ spend energy. By way of contrast, 508 is made from the stems of the horsetail plant (a plant made up entirely of roots and stems without leaves). Moreover, the horsetail is a plant that contains a phenomenal amount of silica, which conducts the upstreaming cosmic forces, balancing the earthly, spreading, watery growth of leaves.

There is also the question of what planetary influences 508 represents. Between the hardening and holding back of the moon's watery influences and the 508's effect in ensuring an abundance of the cosmic forces, it is clear, at least to me, that it represents Saturn. Saturn is the opposite member of the solar family to the moon, and represents both restraint and warmth, and is noted as a channel for cosmic influences.

Using BD 508

BD 508 may be sprayed directly on the soil or on the foliage of plants much the same as 501. Because it is a cosmic polarity preparation like the 501, it should be sprayed in the morning as the dew rises. Certain crops such as lettuce or tomatoes, which have a strong tendency to grow too lush and watery, are commonly treated with 508 even in transplant beds or nursery flats. When there have been repeated heavy rains at or just prior to full moons, 508 may need to be applied to the whole farm.

I spray the 508 on the outside of my compost piles, or I sprinkle a generous pinch of crushed, dried horsetail over the top. I probably need to do this much more in rainy years than in dry ones. In any event, this seems to have made anywhere from a fivefold to a tenfold increase in energy in my compost piles.

Also, dowsing for the potency, I use homeopathic 508 along with 501 in the well of my Cosmic Pipe.

BD Barrel Compost

It was found that BD 500 tended to produce better results on land that had received compost made with the 502 through 507. But, compost is always at a premium, and especially when treating new land or converting a new farm to biodynamic management, there may be no compost available to spread. Clearly some economical and speedy method of applying the 502-507 was needed.

Several early European biodynamic farmers made special composts in boxes or barrels that could be applied homeopathically to fields in similar fashion to 500. In particular Maria Thun refined and popularized a recipe for making barrel compost that makes use of cow manure, basalt powder, eggshell and the compost preps. It has proven very effective as a means of applying the compost preps to large acreages, and has become a standard biodynamic field spray.

Making BD Barrel Compost

To begin with, a wooden barrel (the egg-shaped curvature of a barrel is preferred) without a top or bottom is buried to within six inches of its top in a well-drained location where the soil is fertile and deep—similar to where one might bury BD 500. If one uses a barrel previously used for wine, whiskey, pickles or other preserved products, it should be thoroughly cleaned. I currently am using an oaken whiskey barrel with the top knocked out and filled with water to the brim, along with throwing in a shovelful of compost and stirring. After soaking it for a week, I emptied it out and scrubbed its charred interior with a steel wire brush and wood ashes. Then I filled it again and let it set, throwing in a large bunch of fresh stinging nettles. When this began to smell really rank, I used this nettle tea to water tomato plants and rinsed the barrel out well. I covered it to shade the interior and waited until a pale violet fungus grew on the inside walls. According to Maria Thun this indicates it is ready for use. I then knocked the bottom out of the barrel and buried it where I wanted to make my barrel compost.

Ingredients and Procedures

The principal ingredient of barrel compost is cow (bovine) manure. My barrel is the 50 gallon size, so I collect ten five gallon buckets of fresh manure to make a batch. I empty the manure into a pile in the metal bed of my pickup truck, but a cleanly swept concrete floor is just as good.

To this pile I add 4.5 pounds of powdered basalt (or granite) which amounts to embryonic, new soil. The powdered basalt came from Courtney, who, I believe, got it from someplace in New England, perhaps Vermont.

I also add 14 ounces of eggshell powder which I make from my own chickens' eggs by drying out the shells and saving them to run through my Corona mill. The eggshell material not only adds lime, which is important in combatting the effects of acid rain, but the form of calcium it contains is helpful in protecting from radioactive strontium 90.

The manure plus the rock and eggshell powders are triturated (potentized) before going into the barrel. I use a shovel and pick up scoops of this moist, fresh (doughy, not sloppy) manure at the edge of the pile, dumping them on the top. When the pile is mounded high, I work it down by rapidly shaving off thin, vertical slices with the shovel as though I were mixing up a rather stiff batch of mortar for laying stones. I work around the pile, scooping up manure from the edges and building it up on the top. Then I work it down again all around the sides. This is done quite energetically for a full hour without stopping. It helps to have a friend sharing this labor, and to play music (preferably not rock), sing or something of the sort to make the work proceed rhythmically and easily.

Once the pile is potentized, the manure can be placed in the barrel. However, it is undesirable to pack it so firmly that air cannot penetrate. What I have done is make a frame with half inch mesh hardware cloth in the bottom and a plywood backing that is cut out to be slightly smaller than the top of the barrel. With gloves on, I work the manure through the screen so that it falls into the barrel in crumbs with air space between particles. Of course, this screening is also a further potentization process.

Once the barrel is filled six holes may be made in the material with a stick, so that the 502-507 may be inserted as they would be in an ordinary compost pile. The 502 through 506 are made into pellets and dropped down separate holes, with the 504 and 505 placed in the middle and the others around the edges of the barrel. Each hole should be covered as it is filled. My dowsing indicates that for my barrels it is more effective if I place the 502, 503, 506 and 507 around the outside of the barrel rather than inside it. This gets the best results for me. Commonly however, the preps are all inserted into the manure in the barrel.

The 507 is diluted in a gallon of water and potentized for 15 minutes. This may be a lot of liquid to pour into one hole, and, as with a compost pile, about half may be sprayed on the surface of the barrel and over the surrounding area nearby. Usually I do not do this. Instead I moisten a bit of manure with 20 to 25 drops of 507 and simply drop it down the hole for the 507.

The barrel is then covered with a lid of some sort, usually a sheet of slate or a piece of plywood with a rock on top for weight. While I do not know if it is advisable in dry climates, in my area, where we frequently get 70 inches annual rainfall, I sprinkle 508 over the lid of the barrel. There should be a little air circulation between the atmosphere and the contents, but sunshine and rainwater should be kept out. In a few months the barrel compost, at least the material near the top, should be ready. It should be dark and humusy like good 500.

The first few times I made barrel compost the manure was too moist. I had to remove it from the barrel and let it dry out for a couple days on a sheet of plywood before screening it back into the barrel with a new set of preps. I have made a couple similar batches since, especially when using the sloppy manure that occurs in the spring when the cows are first on green pasture again. The manure simply had to be dried out before it was suitable for composting in a barrel.

Spring and autumn may be the best seasons for making barrel compost, since microbial activity is greatest during these times of the year. However, I start most of my barrels in the winter because I have more time then. Commonly in the spring I screen a full barrel over into an empty barrel, thus "turning" my barrel compost. Ms.

Thun's research in regard to the astrological phenomena indicated that days when the moon or planets were at their nodes are to be avoided in the making of barrel compost. The *Kimberton Hills Agricultural Calendar,* which is published with the biodynamic practitioner in mind, can be used to determine which days should be avoided.

Using BD Barrel Compost

With barrel compost, approximately a third of a cup (65 or 70 grams, or 2.3 ounces by weight) of barrel compost is diluted in three gallons of water and dynamized (potentized) for twenty minutes to cover an acre of land. Stirring is done the same way as with 500 in a crock, bucket, barrel or large cylindrical tank, and sprayed in the late afternoon. (See Chapter IX.) If applied with radionic field unit such as a cosmic pipe, it should be buried a couple of inches below the surface on the east side of the pipe (along with the BD 500) so as to be picked up by the ground level coil.

Energy Balancing Procedure

In the late 80s Hugh Courtney began experimenting with how to apply the BD preps to large areas with minimal delay. He believed that in two days time all the preps could be applied. He tested this out on his farm in Woolwine, Virginia, and later introduced his method at workshops in various parts of the country.

The first afternoon he stirred and applied 500. The next morning he stirred and applied 501. That afternoon he followed up with barrel compost, and the next morning with 508. The idea was that the downworking activity of the 500 would be balanced by the upworking activity of the 501, and the downworking activity of the barrel compost would likewise be balanced by the upworking activity of the 508. He called this an energy balancing procedure.

Especially during the late 80s in the southeastern U.S. there were repeated summertime droughts. Interestingly, wherever this sequence of spraying was employed it was followed within 48 hours by at least technical precipitation if not outright rain. Courtney explained this by saying that the preps had the power to attract whatever was needed, and his experiments indicated that best success in terms of making rain could be expected if the sequence was completed at the time of full moon when the watery forces were strongest.

I explain it a little differently, having investigated Wilhelm Reich's work with rainmaking. I do not think it in any way contradicts Courtney's explanation.

It was one of Reich's observations that drought was always accompanied by stagnant atmospheric conditions. He found that during times of drought the ether would become congested with what he termed DOR (deadly orgone energy). Under high DOR conditions, regardless of the humidity, clouds had trouble forming and rain would not fall. Much of Reich's research in the early 50s was devoted to discovering how to clear out toxic atmospheric conditions and restore a healthy dynamism to the ether, as this would result in regular cycles of rainfall.

My experience with the energy balancing procedure was this. There had been four weeks of stifling, hot weather in late June and early July of 1990. The sky was brown and hazy, but despite humidity readings above 90%, we had no rain and not even any hopeful cloud formation. This is typical of what Reich called DOR. I treated the farm with the energy balancing procedure, and followed it up with morning and evening radionic treatments of the same prep sequence, using the aerial photo of the farm and homeopathic potencies of the preps. On the second afternoon we got a light sprinkle, but by the fourth evening from beginning the spray sequence the DOR had diminished enough that we got cloud formation and a good shower. By the time the radionic treatments had gone a week we were having abundant rain. Again in September the stagnant atmospheric conditions returned and I again resorted to the energy balancing procedure. We rapidly returned to healthy atmospheric conditions where the dew fell heavily at night and burned off quickly in the morning, and we had rain about every fourth day on the average. From that September in 1990 I continued treating the farm radionically with the sequence, 500, 501, barrel compost, 508 and back to 500 again until mid-August of 1991 when we had a small flood at our southeast biodynamic conference. I might add that an area of a hundred mile radius seemed to be affected.

With one exception when Mercury was retrograde, in every case of dry weather when I have used the energy balancing procedure rain has followed in a few days. Of course, I have only experimented on one farm, and that for only a few years. I realize drought conditions may be much more entrenched in parts of the world where rain traditionally is scarce, and I would not suppose this procedure would result in as much rain in Arizona as in Georgia. But it is of interest nonetheless. In every case it cleared up atmospheric stagnation and restored a healthy atmosphere. By the second day of spraying the haze in the atmosphere lessened and cloud formation was much more distinct. By the day after the sequence was completed weather fronts which previously had skirted the region were moving through it, resulting in rain followed by clear, clean skies. Whenever the haze returned I took this as a sign that more of the energy balancing procedure was needed.

This seems an applied example of the dictum of fluid dynamics (sometimes called the butterfly effect by weather forecasters) that a microscopic change at a point can effect large scale changes in the medium. I would like to see others experiment with this procedure.

Homeopathic Milk and Honey

Not all biodynamic farms are flowing with milk and honey, but it could hardly be a bad idea. Milk and honey are, according to spiritual science, foods with special nutritive properties. Milk is especially supportive of growth and development of the etheric (life) body, the astral body and the ego, whereas honey is especially supportive of maturing and refining these.

After an infant reaches the age of two mothers generally wean them and substitute milk from cows or goats instead. Milk processing is a problem, however, as pasteurization (especially flash pasteurization) and homogenization denature milk and rob it of its beneficial forces. But, at least if fresh raw milk is available (as it is likely to be on biodynamic farms) it is very nourishing for children throughout their growth years.

As a person grows they also mature. Honey aids maturation. The maturing process does not stop with the cessation of physical growth, of course, and people may eat honey to good effect way up into old age. Honey is the most refined of plant juices and has been predigested, concentrated and stored in hexagonal, crystal-like, honeycomb cells. Unquestionably it is at its peak of flavor and nutrition in the comb, and if it is extracted it is best raw. Heating or other processing methods pretty much denature honey as they do milk. Honey strengthens the will and the ego body, especially when the etheric and astral bodies have already gotten a good start from milk.

Having a land flowing with milk and honey is a Biblical idea that implies a countryside rich in nourishment for the whole human being, both physically and spiritually. Once the thought occurs, it is obvious homeopathy to spray the fields with diluted and potentized milk and honey.

I credit Hugh Courtney for presenting the idea. I do not know where he got it, but it seems a good idea even though so far I have sprayed my farm with milk and honey only once as a follow up to the 500, 501, barrel compost and 508 sequence. Since it is my purpose in farming to provide food that is as nourishing as possible for the entire human being, I expect to continue to apply this method. Maybe in ten years I can say something about its effects, but I can hardly hold back the idea from others who might wish to try it. Certainly this farm flows with milk and honey.

It is my sense that growth occurs in the evening and at night, and that the milk potency, which I associate with growth, should be sprayed in the evening as with the 500 and barrel compost. For an acre, something like a pint of milk can be added to three gallons of water, potentized for twenty minutes and sprayed in the late afternoon. These quantities can be multiplied for larger acreages.

As for the honey, I have the sense of things like fruits and grains maturing with the Sun and during the daytime, so I think the honey might best be sprayed as with the 501 and the 508. For an acre I would use something like an ounce and a half of honey to three gallons of warm water, again potentized for twenty minutes and sprayed in the early morning.

Weed, Insect, and Animal Peppers

There is still the question of how does the biodynamic grower control weeds, insects and animal pests. Up to now we have dealt only with medicines to regulate and improve dynamic biological activities. We have said nothing about what may be done when one or another species has run amok and threatens to overwhelm us. A few weeds here or there, a few cabbage worms, or an occasional field mouse should be tolerable. Diversity of species is characteristic of thriving ecologies. But sometimes plagues occur, and a species will reproduce to the point it threatens to take over. What can be done?

Whatever it is, it should be simple, economical and beneficial, as well as effective. In other words it must work in harmony with nature and the self-sufficient farm organism.

Weeds

Weeds reproduce and become obnoxious more than anything because of the lunar influences. Because the Moon relates so much to water, we can see this especially in wet years when weeds are much more prevalent than in dry years. Nature provides in fire the force to counter what in water encourages growth and reproduction.

We can go through the fields and save pinches of the seeds of the various weeds that are too abundant. We may get as much as a double handful of all the different kinds, total. These are burned, preferably in a wood flame. The ash is collected and ground up finely with a mortar and pestle until it resembles very fine pepper. In fact, we could simply put it in a pepper shaker and walk about sprinkling a dash here or there. For better results, however, we may homeopathically dilute it out to a potency (usually 7x or 8x) and use it as a field spray and a radionic reagent. Only a little is needed to cover large areas.

By burning the seeds of a plant--or if there are no seeds, the part of the plant that reproduces it, such as the roots--we can bring about a repulsion rather than an attraction for the lunar growth forces on the part of that species without affecting the others around it. The effectiveness of this has been demonstrated even on perennial plants such as the dandelion.

It may make some difference what phase and constellation the Moon is in at the time of burning the seeds or spraying the fields. This is not going to totally eliminate weeds in the first year, but the effects are cumulative, and the second or third year will be more effective. I have never completely eradicated any given weed, though I put lamb's quarters in my weed peppers three years running and ended up not having enough of this delicious weed to eat. I left my local wild amaranth out of my weed pepper a couple years in a row and it went crazy. It was a pest, so I am collecting it for weed pepper again. These are both weeds that love fertile well-balanced soils, and they may have to be controlled one way or the other.

Presumably one could go whole hog and wipe out any given species, but I am too much in favor of diversity to endorse this approach. Just taking a relaxed attitude, if the weed becomes scarce it will be hard to find seeds to burn. If it is easy to find seeds perhaps it needs to be included in the pepper. Two exceptions I can think of, smartweed and galinsoga, are very common on my farm, but I have trouble gathering their seeds. I think I just need to do a better job of gathering.

Insects

For the invertebrates such as insects, it is not simply a matter of the lunar forces. The Sun, as it passes from the constellation of Aquarius around to Cancer, is the key to the growth and reproduction of these animals. This influence is strongest when the Sun is in Taurus. Thus it is optimum to collect insect specimens and burn them to ash when the Sun is in Taurus. Adult insects may be burned on the Aries side of Taurus, while immature insects may be burned on the Gemini side. The ash is then ground and a spray made to treat the problem area. A similar folklore organic method that works on the same principle is to blend insects up in a blender and spray this where the insect in question is not wanted.

I have carried out this procedure with great success in eliminating aphids. I have not done so well with houseflies and cabbage worms. I have needed to try this out on Mexican bean beetles, which are nearly overwhelming some years, but I always seem to be too busy in May and June when the Sun is in Taurus to do this properly.

Potencies in Quantity

I might mention something about making up homeopathic potencies for field spraying, though. A mother tincture is made with approximately three grams of ash to nine tenths ounces of water and succussed for three minutes. Then the first potency (1x) is made by using a tenth ounce of the mother tincture and nine tenths ounces of water and succussing for three minutes. For each further potency the preceding potency is used and the dilution and succussion procedure is the same as long as only one ounce of the potency is desired. But, what if one wants enough of a potency to spray a couple acres or more?

At some point prior to producing the potency desired the quantities must be multiplied. Supposing I wanted to spray the largest of my market garden fields which is nearly three acres, 1,000 ounces (nearly eight gallons) of 8x bean beetle pepper would do the job. I would need to take my entire ounce bottle of 5x and add it to 9 ounces of water in a quart jar or bottle, succussing for three minutes to make the 6x. Adding that 10 ounces of 6x to 90 more ounces of water in a gallon jug I would succuss this for three minutes for my 7x. Adding the 100 ounces of 7x to 900 more ounces of water in a large stirring vessel and stirring it like BD 500 for 20 minutes I would have 1,000 ounces (nearly 8 gallons) of 8x bean beetle pepper ready to be sprayed on my field. It is not really all that hard, and if fractional quantities are desired the mathematics can be worked out along the lines given here.

For instance, a biodynamic dairy farm with a 28 acre field of alfalfa might want to mix up 10,000 ounces (78.1 gallons) of 8x alfalfa weevil pepper in two batches of 39 gallons apiece (depending on the size of the stirring equipment). They could start multiplying their quantities at the 4x stage and when they reached the point they had 1,000 ounces of 7x this could be divided into halves to be combined as 500 ounces to 4,500 ounces of water for each of the 39 gallon batches of 8x.

Higher Animals

With the vertebrates the situation is again different. The key to their prosperity is the planet Venus, particularly in the constellation of Scorpio and particularly when Venus is on the far side of the Sun from the Earth. Here we need no more than the hide of the animal, whether it is a field mouse, a groundhog, a snake or a bird. Steiner indicated that for best results one must obtain this hide and burn it during the high conjunction of Venus with Scorpio.

The way I understand this, Venus may be between the Sun and the Earth (inferior conjunction) at times and at other times it may be on the far side of the Sun from the Earth (superior conjunction). At least in my lifetime neither inferior nor superior conjunction will occur when Venus is in Scorpio, but Venus may be in Scorpio (for brief periods) in some years when it is on the far side of the Sun from us, and in other years (again for brief periods) when it is on the near side of the Sun with us. Only two or three times a decade is it really that far on the far side of the Sun from us when it is in Scorpio, so there is not a lot of opportunity to make this kind of preparation in its most effective form.

My experience is that results, even if not the best results, may be obtained by securing the skin or pelt at whatever time possible even if Venus is not in Scorpio. Then when Venus is in Scorpio even if it is not the high conjunction, ash the skin, grind the ashes up with a mortar and pestle, and make homeopathic potencies.

The peskiest varmint in my market garden is the groundhog. The valley the farm lies in is infested with these critters and they love peas, beans, cabbages and lettuce above all else. I have a groundhog pepper I use on them, and though it may not be the greatest, when I spray the 8x on an area they leave it alone for about a week. It is always the youngest groundhogs that come back first, but at least my pepper works well enough that I get a reasonable return on what I plant. I am looking for that day, however, that I make a better groundhog pepper and can spray it up and down the ridges and creekbanks and get somewhat more long-lasting relief.

In this connection availability of good quality animal pepper potencies probably ought to be established, and if you make a good one you might communicate about it to BD Preps in Woolwine, Virginia.

BD Tree Paste

Peter Escher developed this as a method of strengthening the bark of fruit trees, since that is one of their weaker points. Starting with a heavy clay such as bentonite, this is mixed with a little water, which may be in the form of stirred BD 500, barrel compost or any particularly appropriate preps. To this add some finely ground lime and some linseed oil and stir well. The result should be about the consistancy of paint and can be applied once or twice a year to the first foot or so of bark on fruit trees.

A homeopathic potency series made from groundhog skin burned to ash when Venus was in Scorpio, ground to powder and diluted and potentized to 7x.

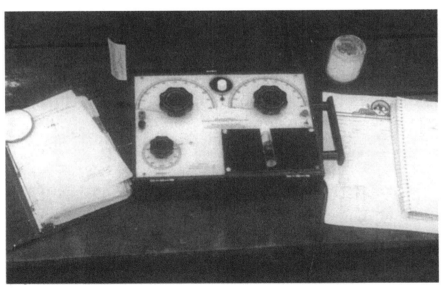

A genuine Hieronymus analyzer. This is one of the most reliable radionic analysis and treatment devices.

Chapter XII

One of the purposes of biodynamic agriculture is to lay the foundations for a healthier, more stable society. This requires seeing farming in the cultural perspective of human society. Second only to good farming practices and use of the BD preps, the concept of a threefold social order is key to establishing healthy BD farms. In other words we need to know where we are, where we are coming from and where we are going.

As a whole, society is made up of three parts--the economic, political and significance spheres. This parallels the individual who is made up substantially of guts, heart and head, and essentially of will, feeling and thought.

Such awarenesses do not enter the social mainstream all at once. Rather they evolve into it over the course of generations.

At the time of the American Revolution it was recognized that we were better off keeping politics and religion separate. Nonetheless there was a failure to see that science, philosophy, religion and the arts were all essentially significant in nature. Much worse, there was a failure to realize that economics must not dominate either politics or religion--that regardless of their integral working they must all three stand on their own.

This is fine idealism, but it is difficult to keep government from meddling with religious matters, to say nothing about keeping religious groups from meddling in politics--as witness the prayer and abortion issues. Moreover, military research threatens that science and technology will dominate political and economic events just as much as it threatens that political or economic interests will dictate to science and technology. Meanwhile, justified by Keynesian economics, governments enter into the economic domain and raise huge revenues on income and sales taxes, thus striking at the heart of economic activity. This ignores the fact that along with protection of life, the protection of property (and hence taxation of property) are the main political imperatives. As if to add insult to injury, governments make public education their domain even though the quest for knowledge, truth and the development of ability is essentially significant in nature.

Above all, economic forces influence the political sphere. Money determines the outcome of elections. It is unrealistic to imagine the press is free no matter that government and special interests do not (openly) interfere. Huge sums are required to publish and broadcast for mass consumption, and those who pay determine the agenda. Big companies with millions to spend popularize ideas like "bigger is better" and "cure your problems by buying a product." The ideas of "small is beautiful" and "prevention is the best medicine" receive comparatively little press.

In political campaigns in a two or three way race the smart money goes to all the top candidates. Otherwise they would not be top candidates. Thus the election process does the bidding of those who have money. The so-called political issues that the press covers are little more than window dressing. The persuasion of the media is more all-pervasive than practically anyone imagines. Just by repeatedly portraying political leaders and credentialed experts as dealing with the world's problems the masses are brainwashed into accepting that these people have the only solutions to our problems, while in reality they tend to be allied with the causes. The media would have us think that as individuals we are helpless and a man of integrity can not take his life into his own hands and address all issues in an immediate and everyday way through his choices of action or inaction.

Of course, it cannot be said that the economic sphere as a whole controls the political sphere, any more than it would be true to say the political sphere as a whole controls production and consumption, despite income and sales taxes. Relatively few people within the economic sphere exert any guiding influence, and even this for the most part is concealed, as follows.

Economics is made to seem so mysterious that most people throw up their hands and leave it to the professionals. There are complicated formulas for calculating gross national product, rate of inflation, money supplies, consumer price indexes, etc., so that the ordinary individual does not know what is going on. This allows the experts to run things unchallenged. This they do, starting with the reality that as the division of labor increases, we develop greater capacity to produce abundantly. Economists point out that this capacity to produce would upset the status quo unless by taxation it is held back and expended on such things as military or welfare programs. Thus the political lines are drawn so that those inclined to think they are liberal are pro social spending and anti-military. Those thinking they are conservative are pro-defense and anti-welfare handouts, as though there could be no one who did not approve of one or the other reasons for eliminating abundance. No one gets around to questioning why we must not be allowed to produce abundantly.

My first curriculum in college was business, and this cured me of a number of illusions. I quickly grasped the fact that as we developed faster and more efficient means of production we could produce far more than ever before. But, strangely, more and more American parents were both working for paychecks while getting deeper and deeper into debt. To unravel the counter-intuitive logic of this I learned how money comes into existence, how it disappears, how it relates to real wealth, the causes for inflation, what generates buying power, and the cyclical nature of economic upsets. In short I learned the game by which the status quo perpetuated itself.

Savings become worthless if not put to good use. But those who save would hardly do so if they had a use for the money saved. Banks put savings to work. Nearly all banks pay interest for savings left on deposit, while loaning this money out again at a higher rate of interest. The interest system by nature assumes that money on deposit or out on loan will double every so many years as interest is compounded. This ends up flying in the face of nature, to say nothing of Mosaic law.

Nature allows things to grow only to their limits. Then they must decline. Interest systems make no allowance for this, leaving it up to inflation and bankruptcy. Neither of these is satisfactory to its victims. Economies tied to the interest game typically go through massive inflations and bankruptcies every fifty-five to sixty years, and the last time we had this situation in America was the early nineteen thirties. Moses knew this thousands of years ago.

When money is loaned at interest, the money supply must increase if the amount required to repay loans is not to end up exceeding the total in circulation. In our present economy these increases in money supply are commonly generated by new debt, both public and private. The banking system not only lends out the bulk of its deposits, but, based on the estimated strength of loan portfolios, we have a central bank which pyramids lending even further. However, debt can balloon only so far before natural laws intervene.

Ordinarily loans are secured by claims on property as collateral. A certain percentage of defaults are expected, and if a loan goes into default the property is taken over by the lenders and sold. However, a time must come when defaults run high enough that there is too much property and not enough buyers. Then property in default is either not sold, or it is sold for less than the amount outstanding on the loans, and banks collapse. To keep the economy *going without serious upheaval, the rate of bankruptcies must be paced so that it does not get too far out of hand. This is the job of the central bank, in this case the Federal Reserve, a private corporation given the aura of government authority.*

On the other hand, raw material production is the natural counterbalance of this lending game. As most raw materials are agricultural, farms are the main starting places for generation of real wealth. Most other economic activities derive in one or more ways from agriculture. After all, money is not worth any more than what you can spend it for. Abundance of farm commodities is basic to a wealthy society, and if there is a serious shortage it may not matter how much money one has.

One of the things implied in this is that the monetary value of agricultural products is the chief measure of the economy's earned income. If agricultural prices are kept as low as possible there is not much earned income. Who would favor this? As too much earned income would pay off loans and put the banking business into eclipse, this is the agenda of banks.

In a nutshell, whoever controls agricultural production controls the world economy. This is why the international dealers in grain (also the largest depositors in banks), under the guise of "free trade" have worked so hard to eliminate all obstacles to their manipulation of world commodity markets. This also is why worldwide elimination of broad based independent, self-sufficient, (family) farms has long been the intent of those who work to control the world.

At the turn of the twentieth century 90% of Americans came from family farms. People generated earned income and there was little debt. Now fewer than three percent farm. Correspondingly, today farmers generate little earned income and the American economy is awash in debt.

In fact, due to bankruptcies, the Federal Reserve is in the position of being the largest absentee landlord in America. Nor is the U.S. government an example of fiscal responsibility. It is over its eyebrows in debt to the Fed, a privately owned corporation. It is hard to imagine these debts all being repudiated. That is the sort of thing wars are made of, and we will have to consider that the wealthiest Arabs and Asians are amongst the largest owners of U.S. government debt paper. I'm unsure of the exact picture aside from the fact that most Arab and Japanese trade surpluses are locked into long term investments in a variety of stocks, bonds and lending enterprises, including U.S. treasury bonds.

Of course, Americans are by no means the only ones caught up in this colonialism of debt. We may be able to see it better by looking at the the global picture.

Asia was in large part colonized by force of European arms. But, Mohandas Gandhi showed the limitations inherent in this. To ensure that debt took the place of subjugation by force in Asia, the four thousand year old self-sufficiency of Asian family farmers had to be undermined. Large scale, debt ridden agriculture along the lines of the American model was the agenda.

In some parts of Asia the terrain and the political situations lent themselves to large scale farming. In some parts these did not. In the latter corrupt governments were fostered, the countryside chafed under its tax burdens, internal wars were fomented and family farms turned into wastelands.

Even as we bombed Viet Nam, Cambodia and Laos into oblivion, agricultural development projects were designed and funded in more favorable locations by the world's largest lenders. Mechanized competition for the Japanese (and ultimately the Chinese) market drove the small scale family farmers of India, Pakistan, Bangladesh, Indonesia, Burma and elsewhere to either become cogs in a vast agricultural machine, or leave their land for city jobs.

Methods that depended heavily on industry, technology and the world grain trade were a requirement for approval of loans by the Asian Development Bank and Fund (which despite the name was an extension of world banking).

In Sri Lanka, for instance, the peasants rather naively embraced the new way and it became the thing to shoot your water buffalo. In the rich, mountainous district of Baggio in the Philippines this did not go over. So instead Baggio's farms were flooded by a gigantic hydroelectric project.

Governments were influenced in a variety of ways to support the new agricultural agenda, which was heralded as a "green revolution." While the agricultural loans were being handed out, many governments further entangled themselves in debt for a variety of military, industrial and social projects.

The new, large scale agricultural projects greatly reduced the number of farm workers required to produce large volumes, so they could not absorb any significant portion of the food they produced. They were forced to sell virtually all of their production to international buyers, flooding the market and weakening prices. Statistics showed that far more rice was entering trade channels than ever before. Hence it was claimed that rice production had greatly increased. But the millions of dispossessed peasants, now living in cities virtually from hand to mouth no longer had a year's supply of rice at harvest time. They were lucky to have a week's supply, and even then all of this came through trade channels. Where previously large numbers of peasants produced their own rice, now they depended on buying it. There was more rice traded all right, because far fewer people were growing their own. If anything, in reality there was less rice produced. So much for statistics and for what statistics can prove.

This same game plan was employed in Africa and South America. Coffee cooperatives were set up where fertilizers and toxic chemicals were a requirement for growers who wanted to sell their crops. Sugar plantations, fishing and forestry, palm oil, rubber, coconut and banana projects, all were designed, funded and set into motion by a world banking hegemony pursuing its colonialism. For the most part this was of no benefit either to the ecology or the people driven into the cities from the countryside.

There was a lot of propaganda about how the world bank and the international monetary fund were developing agricultural production for the benefit of the third world. But, the truth is this was a worldwide power grab--at the expense of rain forests, agricultural self-sufficiency, and most of all people and human dignity.

It might as well be pointed out that the peasants of Asia, Africa and South America, driven into the cities in search of jobs, have undercut American laborers. Large numbers of jobs have been exported overseas where people must work more cheaply.

This is what centralization of authority and the bigger is better mindset led to. It kept the production of wealth to a minimum, monetizing debt instead of production. Humanity was left with a precarious existence as wage slaves. Key to this process was the elimination of self-sufficient family farms, worldwide.

If we want to turn the tables we need to take a good look at the relationship between economics and agriculture. Then we may be prepared in the future to invent a society where people exercise freedom because they assume responsibility. Our alternative is to lapse into slavery and, ultimately, extinction. The really worthwhile things--quality nutrition, a healthy environment, personal initiative, the knowledge of doing something beneficial for all and avoiding useless and destructive activities--will be lost.

"We cannot be free if our food sources are controlled by someone else."
—Wendell Berry

Economics and Agriculture

The production of food from the natural elements is the fundamental economic activity that supports everything else. Reciprocally, an understanding of economic realities goes hand in hand with creating an approach to farming that takes responsibility for how its actions affect the whole.

Of course, if we travel in conventional circles we might think that agriculture has little to do with economics. It is as though farmers should concentrate on sowing and harvesting, and leave economics to the Ph.D.s. Our faith in specialization tends to persuade us we should compartmentalize our treatment of both agriculture and economics.

Specialization

Specialization has its virtues. If one person grinds grain and another bakes bread, between them they can provide bread of consistent quality for a community of people herding sheep, making shoes, building, weaving, recycling junk and so forth. Specialization allows individuals to develop their unique talents, abilities and interests, saving much time, energy and materials in the process.

In a medieval township of one or two thousand people, the economic function of each individual was fairly evident. One saw production arise out of nature and consumption return this to nature.

With the advent of the industrial revolution people gathered into cities and concentrated on using their specialties to earn money. A lathe operator, for instance, might work from technical drawings without concern about optimum design. Nor need he worry about assembly, marketing, repair or recycling. Being a master at his specialty was sufficient to keep him occupied. The printing press designer did not run printing presses as an occupation. He had no need to get twenty hours worth of printing done in eighteen. He might never wish this or that lever or screw was easier to operate or harder to maladjust. He specialized in design and left it up to pressmen to run the thing.

Increasingly generations were born, educated, worked and died without understanding how their activities fitted into the economy as a whole. As they lost sight of how their contributions influenced society, they lost their ability to judge the benefits or dangers of their actions. The result was they performed tasks they would not have considered had they understood the consequences from start to finish. In short, specialization was a good thing that, taken to the extreme, ultimately became automatic, inappropriate, even hazardous.

For instance, at the beginning of the industrial revolution the English estate holders specialized in grazing sheep and producing wool. They implemented enclosure acts that sent the peasants off to the cities creating a surplus labor pool. This was exploited by mills that manufactured woolen goods for export. In the overall this was socially catastrophic, but an economic bonanza for a few.

Quixotically it gave rise to the English custom of maintaining closely clipped lawns around houses rather than well-tended vegetable, herb and flower gardens--an effort to copy the look of the affluent estates with their sheep trimmed grounds. Today, by way of trying to achieve this cultural ideal, Americans go to extraordinary lengths to maintain mock pastures, filling up landfills with the residues from riding lawnmowers and herbiciding the dandelions instead of growing food.

Environmental Consequences

Traditionally farmers have as close a connection as anyone to watching products arise out of nature and return as waste. They might not see what the governor or academic does with the fruits of agriculture, but at least they tend to know where and how basic commodities arise. Still, the industrial revolution, despite the obvious benefits of increased specialization, blindsided us with various disasters even in agriculture.

Bigger, heavier plows and other machinery brought on increases in soil erosion. Manures were concentrated more while recycling them received less attention. Imbalances, deficiencies, declines and catastrophes became increasingly common. The seed ran out in one district, the soil washed away in another, and a plague killed the crops or the livestock elsewhere. Traditions increasingly were ignored, or followed with insufficient understanding of why they existed.

During the latter part of the nineteenth century, in response to the widespread problem of declining fertility, a renowned chemist, Justus von Liebig, found that small amounts of the salts of nitrogen, phosphorus and potassium boosted plant growth wherever these elements were in short supply. Producers of these chemicals embraced Liebig's discovery, and little attention was paid to the fact that crops grown with these salt fertilizers tended to be watery, weak and subject to pest problems despite their large size or superficial vigor.

With the advent of World War II the production of nitrogen compounds commenced on a tremendous scale in order to meet the demand for explosives. After the war this chemical output was applied to farms, and chemical agriculture became the norm.

Chemical fertilization resulted in a sharp increase in insect and disease problems. In response to this the production and sale of toxic chemicals became big business. For the most part the decline in flavor, nutrition and goodness was glossed over. What was emphasized was quantity, not quality. Because they were themselves narrowly focused specialists, few consumers had any idea what was going on.

Fertilizer producers founded institutes and lobbied, passing laws favoring their wares. They set up networks for research and advice that assured the most widespread acceptance. Where once farmers had burned and pulverized stones, rotated crops, recycled manures and maintained a close contact with their land to achieve sound results, specialization made these things seem obsolete.

In reality, however, both agriculture and the economy were closed systems where everything arose from nature and inevitably in one way or another returned. The progression from heavier plows to salt fertilizers to toxic rescue chemistry was a classic case of the pitfalls of specialization. Blind to the overview, we eroded soils, impoverished root growth and microbial activity, polluted the air and water and seriously compromised the quality of our food supply. Hi-tech agriculture damaged the ecology at the same time that it locked farmers into a high-cost/must sell situation with a heavy load of debt.

In a village of one or two thousand people it would have been inconceivable to use such short-sighted methods of producing basic foods. But farmers no longer ate their own crops. Instead they purchased food from supermarkets, and out of sight was out of mind. Toxic agriculture became routine. The roles of earthworms, ants, wasps, bees and other contributors were ignored while one farmer specialized in corn and soybeans, another in rice and sugarcane.

Before World War II animal fats, though they would have concentrated toxic residues had these been in the food chain, were considered healthy fare. In the 1990s, however, regardless of the cholesterol theory, toxic residues ensure that eating high fat animal products may be a prelude to cardiac by-pass surgery, kidney dialysis or a cancer operation.

To understand the extent to which specialization has us in its grip we might graph the share of the world economy devoted to medical treatment over the past hundred fifty years as compared to topsoil losses over the same period. While it might seem common sense that public health is closely related to the vitality of soils and crops, in today's specialized world it is common to hear the medical associations denying any relationship between declining nutritional values, soil loss, agricultural toxicity and health problems.

Yet, it is no accident that we have a health care crisis simultaneous with the debasement of our agriculture. We have less humus in our soils than ever, too much crude nitrogen, and a deficiency of oxygen. We have bred most crops to depend solely on soluble chemistry rather than soil solids, and foods have declined in mineral content. We are malnourished, not only physically (not enough minerals), but also etherically (not enough oxygen), astrally (too much crude nitrogen) and egoically (insufficient carbon in our soils). How have things worsened so rapidly? Something must be driving society relentlessly into the ditch.

To gain an understanding of our situation we must see things as wholes in the context of larger and larger wholes, rather than isolated and compartmentalized as specialization encourages. In reality everything is interconnected and interdependent. We must learn to think holistically.

The Ultimate Specialty

Once money replaced brutality as the chief tool for securing ownership and control, it became the object of power. Accordingly there is probably no one more specialized than the specialist at handling money.

By virtue of holding only a small fraction of deposits, a bank can reissue the rest as loans, doubling and redoubling the money supply since in theory all the money is simultaneously still in the bank. This assumes that only a small fraction of the bank's depositors will want their assets back at any one time, and to shore up this assumption we created a banking regulation agency, the Federal Deposit Insurance Corporation (FDIC) which supposedly guarantees deposits. Thus, by issuing loans, banks create money out of nothing. This is compounded over time at some rate of interest. Accordingly a portion of the income from lending money is paid as interest to depositors. As more and more money is lent and interest mounts up, mature fortunes multiply themselves.

A serious flaw in this system is that if money is to represent wealth it must age and wear out just as do food, clothing, shelter and other items. It is not enough simply to have a medium of exchange, we need a medium of exchange that is grounded in reality--one that encourages exchange so that everyone gets a share, and one that wears out like all the things it represents.

Gold, for instance, may be a stable medium of exchange since it does not multiply itself when hoarded, but it is a false medium of exchange because it does not wear out.

On the other hand, raw materials, especially foods, wear out quickly. Even the most carefully stored grains are likely to last only a decade or so. The world's wealth in these items needs to be replenished constantly. Their production is the basic, true measure of how much wealth exists in any economy. Thus, a dated currency, issued on the basis of raw material production and wearing out over a period of, say, ten years, would stimulate turnover in currency in all sectors of the economy. Before long we would treasure nature, out of which all products flow, instead of amassing savings to be multiplied by a carefully orchestrated need for loans. Then we would avoid the pitfalls of usury.

Usury

In modern times usury has come to mean the lending of money at exorbitant interest. Originally it meant lending at any interest. In the Mosaic tradition usury was forbidden because interest is based on doubling and redoubling mature fortunes, while for the ordinary producer and consumer everything money represents wears out.

Biblical scriptures, particularly Deuteronomy and Leviticus, which are basic to Jewish, Christian and Moslem traditions, prohibit usury as well as the confiscation of family agricultural lands for non-payment of debt. That is something to think about.

Yet, this type of lending is firmly ensconced in the legal codes and political traditions of most of the world today.

Somehow, world around, laws have established usury and courts uphold it as socially virtuous and acceptable. Sheriffs enforce its imperatives with threats, if not actual violence. It is a policy we are conditioned to accept.

Debunking Political Myths

Many believe the voting booths and legislative bodies are a realistic avenue for citizens to voice dissent. And, perhaps they would be if consensus was pursued and citizens represented themselves. However, representative assemblies make it difficult for individuals to have any real voice unless they have plenty of money and influence. Legislative decisions depend on politicians who need campaign contributions to get elected, frequently spending enormously more running for an office than it pays in salary. For instance, roughly half a billion dollars was spent during the 1988 US presidential campaign campaigning for a $250,000 a year job.

Needless to say, if the income from usury is in the trillions annually, a little can be budgeted for political influence, and those with this agenda can afford to back all the top candidates.

Dissent, though it may be voiced in legislatures, is routinely silenced by majority rule, no matter the elegance of its arguments. And, should the lone citizen think to protest in a court of law, his dissent is muzzled and shunted aside by well-practiced manipulations of the legal rubrics. Never mind the Magna Cartas and Declarations of Independence or any other traditions that misgovernment must not be borne.

Moreover, the scions of the media, schools and public institutions would have us believe this system is fair, just, reasonable and the best that has existed in all history. Of course, to suggest otherwise might imperil their job security.

Is the Press Free?

I realize many believe we enjoy freedom of the press, and that by proclaiming the truth the media will enlighten people so that they shake off their enslavement. However, publishing or broadcasting to the masses requires massive funding. The major media are controlled--frequently through advertising budgets or by way of donations to pet projects, charities or cultural pursuits rather than outright ownership. Editors who ignore the wishes of their benefactors seldom last long.

Moreover, propaganda techniques have progressed steadily since the days of the Third Reich. Marketing psychologists have developed sophisticated methods for evaluating the emotions evoked by audio and visual presentations. And, it is emotions that motivate people. Public relations are programed by top professionals who know how to find a way to sell practically anything to any audience. Public opinion is molded by those who pay for it.

What about Science?

Some suppose *science* at least must be free from mummery and manipulation. But, it too is controlled by funding, and as for those who fund their own investigations, there are strong arm tactics.

Roger Gerdeman, an Iowa farm boy whose family funded his work to develop a turbine that took the heat out of air and used it for motive power, was kidnapped by persons posing as FBI agents. He was found wandering the streets of Mexico City, a mental vegetable, with his work lost or stolen.

Dr. Joseph A. Beasley, a Tulane medical professor who operated two clinics, researched and developed a vitamin cure for diabetes. This threatened drug revenues in eleven digits, and he soon found himself tried and convicted of technical improprieties in the use of federal grant monies.

Royal R. Rife, with the financial backing of a bearing manufacturer by the name of Timpken, discovered a way to cure cancer and various other diseases with economical frequency generators--whereupon he was charged with practicing quack medicine and hounded into seclusion in Mexico.

Wilhelm Reich, one of Sigmund Freud's most renowned successors, funded his own research into the basic phenomena of life. After brilliant work concerning reversal of the law of increasing entropy, weather modification and the use of simple equipment to improve personal vitality, Morris Fischbein (simultaneously of the AMA and the Food and Drug Administration) brought Reich to trial for medical quackery. After being pilloried in the media, with his published works and experimental devices destroyed by court order, he died an untimely death in prison.

In this regard things have changed little since the days of Giordano Bruno, who was burned at the stake, and Galileo Galilei, who became a guest of the Inquisition for arguing that the Earth went around the Sun. People in power do their best to control anything which can penetrate to the truth of things, for they know it may rock the boat.

Scientific research, just as with any religious pursuit, has little hope of funding and recognition by the mature fortunes unless it furthers their influence.

Nor is revolution a hopeful avenue of dissent. What is left? Keeping abreast of developments and biding one's time?

The likelihood is that the manipulators who currently pull the strings are essentially specialists of their own kind. They are so wrapped up in their specialty that there is virtually no way for them to perceive the ecological and economical needs of the whole.

Basics

A lot depends on controlling the means for basic production, most of which is agricultural land. For some time control of land has passed into the hands of the mature fortunes and out of the hands of those living on it or working it. So it is the wealthy and powerful who make the key decisions about land use, regardless of whether these are called modern corporate agriculture, FmHA requirements, international monetary fund guidelines, blatant absentee landlordism or agricultural collectivization. In so-called Third World countries, especially those deeply in debt, this trend has been a serious bone of contention for many decades. Yet, few Americans realize how much they themselves have become a dispossessed people. Partly this is a measure of how skillfully they have been manipulated.

There have been many refinements in the process of securing control of the land, and, of course, there have been blunders. Iran, for instance, epitomized a blunder. The Shah moved aggressively to collectivize farm land, moving people into the cities so rapidly that most remembered the independence and self-determinism of their former rural existence. When times got hard they listened to Khoumieni, who promised to turn the clock back.

The American media explained that the Shah had tried to modernize Iran too fast, but few knew what that really meant.

Iran was a culture which had grown its own food for thousands of years. When the Shah bulldozed the small farms with their goat pens, chicken coops and fig trees, feeding their population into the cities, Iran lost its diversified, self-sufficient base, becoming dependent on agricultural imports. Oil or no oil, the economic and ecological changes left people caught between wage slavery and unemployment with no family farm to go back to. Most could remember when it was otherwise.

By way of contrast the process has gone more slowly in America. The majority of the population these days were born and raised by wage earners in the towns and cities. They know almost nothing about living off the land even if they happen to own a little. Thus there is little perceived need for land reform here. In fact, many of those who do work the land maintain the illusion that they own their land and are free to do what they please with it despite their huge debts and dependence on methods that keep them on a treadmill. Whatever independence they might have they relinquish by seeking relief both financially and technologically in programs promoted by the central government.

Centralized Authority

The process is one of centralization of authority. But what are its premises? For one thing it assumes central authority knows what is best for individuals and what they should do. For another it must enforce its decisions. This means having the bureaucrat and the policeman looking over the citizen's shoulder supposedly to make him be responsible. The US, though nominally free, has the world's largest central government, the most laws, the largest enforcement organizations and the highest per capita prison population. This is a consequence of centralization. On the one hand, many people give up being responsible on their own initiative. On the other, many are penalized for attempting to assume such responsibility.

Historically centralized control results in land abuse. Long-range husbandry suffers while a dispossessed population waits to be told what to do. Workers have little say over their economic activities. If they refuse to perform because they think what they are told to do is inappropriate, unsafe, immoral or whatever, they are simply replaced. As "surplus population" they may starve, end up in prison or learn to do as they are told next time.

Government researchers tell us that environmental quality, self-sufficiency and long range environmental improvement are nice ideals, but very difficult to attain and sure to be poor business. But, how can this be? A pure, balanced and natural reaping of nature's bounty is inferior to a toxic, wasteful and extortive approach?

On one hand billions are spent on development and deployment of environmentally destructive food production methods. On the other hand, sound economic environmentalism is left to scattered individuals who reap minimal economic gain while being treated like lunatics. The central authorities promote the belief that the only way we can produce sufficient food is by raping the environment and mortgaging everything. Is it a coincidence that this favors, amongst others, those who have profitable investments in toxic industries?

Propaganda pervades the media, the classrooms and the political arenas. The glitz, color, authority figures and subliminal cues are well-researched, clever and thorough. They go beyond either reasoned argument or simple paid advertising to emotional persuasion, since emotion is more compelling when it comes to peoples' actions. Nearly everyone is conditioned to accept that toxic agriculture is the only way to produce food. In order to get along and not be branded as crazy most people have learned to accept the pillage and desertification of the planet, deplorable though it may be. The propaganda goes down all the more smoothly since at the cultural level the suggestion is implanted early on in life (via cartoons and comic books) that at some point our superheroes will emerge from deep cover and pull all our chestnuts out of the fire for us if we just have faith and go along with the authorities.

Yet, it makes no sense for producers to destroy their production base, endangering their own health and welfare along with future generations. Why is this viewpoint promoted? Who could benefit from the destruction of nature? Tropical forests are cut, temperate forests succumb to acid rain, ocean life is poisoned, the atmosphere is polluted and now we suffer from increased ultraviolet exposure, weather extremes and tectonic instability. Neither producers nor consumers can be said to benefit. Who does?

Who Benefits?

Classically it is the trader's game to dry up abundance and endanger future production. All the better to cash in on goods set aside when there was a surplus, thus gaining a larger war chest and greater leverage in the next trading cycle. Since trading in money trumps all other trading games, money manipulators exercise authority over all aspects of trade.

Producers and consumers are kept as separate as possible. Producers are told there is too much and they must sell cheap, while at the same time consumers are told there is too little and they must pay dear. Both producers and consumers are at the mercy of the markets.

Suppose the American soybean harvest is in and is fairly abundant. The soybean trader cries, "Surplus!" playing those who must sell against each other. He may import foreign beans to drive domestic prices down, then turn around and export domestic production to drive foreign prices down. Ideally he tries to force farmers to accept less than their cost of production while they must meet current financial obligations. This practically ensures that in following years farmers can be pressured even more. And if a significant number of farmers are bankrupted the way is paved for a year of too little production. Then worldwide stockpiles will bring very high prices. The following year or two as soybean production increases in an effort to cash in on higher prices, the trader goes back to crying surplus. The last thing that is wanted is diversified farms that can absorb their own production unless or until they are offered a desirable price.

If there is a drought and the price of feeds go up, the poultry, cattle or hog farmers must sell off their livestock. This drives meat prices down at the same time feed costs soar, a production absurdity, but a trader's delight. He can buy, buy, buy while producers must sell, marketing a portion of this surplus at a very healthy profit when prices rise again because of curtailed production.

In Robin Hood's time the corn engrosser charged twenty shillings for a bushel of barley at planting time. The yeoman farmer had to go to the money lender who fixed the loan to be paid at harvest time. At harvest the corn engrosser paid only one shilling a bushel and the yeoman had to take it if he was going to keep the sheriff off his back. Frequently this meant going back in debt again at planting time. The corn engrosser, the money lender and the sheriff were all fast friends.

Virtually the same story is told about ancient Babylonia. Little has changed although hundreds, even thousands of years have passed. Producers succumb to this fleecing time and again. The salaried experts, funded researchers and farm specialists offer little of use to farmers in this position. Instead they offer more and more products for farmers to buy, locking them into larger crop loans and increased pressure to sell their production cheap. For the trader this is ideal. He prefers to see the farmer forced to sell as this is likely to increase his profits. Moreover, he can place his profits on deposit to earn interest as they are issued out again as loans.

Need for Parity

Reducing the profits of the primary producer not only handicaps his production position, it ensures he must go into debt if he is to consume others' products. The world's strong economies such as Japan and Germany try to ensure their farmers are compensated fairly well, and starvation is uncommon in these countries. Conversely cheap farm export countries such as Brazil and Argentina have weak economies and widespread starvation.

In the US during the forties, with the urgency of a war to fight, parity legislation was enacted to ensure that farm products brought prices to put them on par with non-farm products. Before long farmers and factory workers alike enjoyed increasing prosperity and diminishing debt, a real relief after the thirties.

Then in the fifties farmers again began to be shortchanged. The economy faltered while public and private debts grew again.

The reason is that no matter what the primary producer's output is, if he receives no pay for it he will buy nothing from any of the secondary producers, and so it will run through the economy. Nor would he produce at all the next year and the whole economy would halt. So he is always paid something, but if he receives low pay he will buy less than if he is well paid, and the effects will be felt, even multiplied, throughout the economy. If he is strung along just right he will go deeper and deeper in debt hoping for a good year to get him out, and again the same tendency will prevail, even magnify, throughout the economy as a whole. If he were paid well he would prosper, and that prosperity again would pervade the whole economy and diminish the need for going into debt toward zero, which is not what is on the agenda.

The speed with which money and goods change hands determines how much the basic producer's earnings are multiplied in the economy. Things move so fast these days that even slight earnings can multiply many fold. But if the basic producer has no earnings there is no multiplication to be had, and if he ceases to produce, everyone throughout the economy loses. So, agricultural commodity prices are juggled well enough to tease the economy along without any real prosperity. It remains to be seen how long this can be kept up. The situation is pretty touchy, and global weather extremes alone could throw a monkeywrench into the works.

Remedy

Since the current scheme of things is established and upheld by legislation, government administration and jurisprudence, to say nothing of police, it would seem that remedy would have to be political in nature, a matter of clearing a path for the righting of wrongs. But, how can elected officials, judges, bureaucratic agencies or police resist the influence of money?

It is a sobering fact that John F. Kennedy and Abraham Lincoln were both assassinated after issuing US currency that was not based on debt and payment of interest. Had either of these presidents lived long enough to convert us from currency based on government borrowing to currency based on how much we produced of basic commodities, they would have gotten the country out of debt. They never got the chance. And, in both cases their alleged assassins were killed before they could give testimony or defend themselves in court. It is unlikely they were the real killers.

Other social leaders such as Mohandas Gandhi, Malcolm X, Robert Kennedy and Martin Luther King, Jr. have also been assassinated before they could address these issues. Considering the stakes of the game it seems unhealthy to buck the status quo.

But, if concentrating political authority in the hands of a president, congress and judiciary and its army and police yields no remedy, how are we to maintain a polite society? Scattered individuals cannot simply remain polite while society at large and particularly government itself becomes increasingly impolite. We must do better than this. Our environment and the community of living beings on the Earth (and ultimately throughout the cosmos) is at stake.

Many have suggested that we withdraw our support of the system as it stands. That may be done though it is difficult, but it is not enough. We must put our efforts behind a constructive program.

One of the highest priorities, aside from learning to see clearly and disentangle ourselves from enslavement, is to establish a true economic husbandry of the environment, particularly of agriculture.

This requires developing a personal integrity and farm integrity in relation to the underlying, all-encompassing unity of the Earth and the cosmos, and it requires that we act on our own authority. It also requires support and cooperation, a community effort. It cannot be done in a vacuum.

By engaging in the primary production of wealth, the farmer is in the best position to observe what is a wholesome harvest of nature's gifts and a healthy recycling. It is his challenge to transform the world into one of health and bounty. To do this he must link up with the people who consume his products and contribute in their turn to the quality of life, culture and material wealth that make farming satisfying. Then others will want to join in his work. He must cease dealing with middlemen who reduce his labors to statistics in a global power game, and associate directly with those who desire what he can produce.

This requires reexamining the specialist's view that concentrating on just a few things and doing them well is best. Such a view goes hand in hand with the idea that competition is best, and this manner of thinking has so far carried the day. It has led many farmers into specializing in producing just a few commodities on as large a scale as possible, and not only has this been disastrous for farm ecologies, but it has left these farmers vulnerable to market pressure as never before.

Putting Specialization into Perspective

In the broader scheme of nature diversity is best for survival, and cooperation between species benefits them all. It follows along these lines that a person with multiple talents and abilities is better equipped for survival, and a community made up of the most varied individuals, of the most diverse professions and positions is the best off.

As one neighbor who dairy farms observed, "I don't know what we've got to do, but I know one thing for sure. We need to get more people out here working on our farms."

I agree. If we did and people knew where their food came from and what went into producing it there would be an awakening and more cooperation.

I do not think it will be enough to merely certify products are organically or biodynamically grown, though this may be a step in the right direction. But, whether the farm enterprise is large or small I suspect it is key to communicate where the food came from, who grew it and how, and what is happening on that farm as a whole. With consumers identifying with the farms that feed them and getting involved with the way their food is grown, the middlemen no longer will enjoy an unfair advantage.

Chapter XIII

The word politics comes from the same roots as the word polite. The procedure of counting heads--of polling--is essentially a political and a polite thing to do, and rather incidentally has a thing or two to do with polled cattle having no horns. In a polite society a person can stand up, be counted and have his say.

I realize that we are taught that ours is an age of the greatest political sophistication. But much is left to be desired in terms of politeness in the way government treats the citizens, let alone how the citizens treat each other. Democracy, which children frequently are taught is the form of government we enjoy, has the flaw that it tends to oppress those in the minority. Yet, we do not have a democracy. More than anything we have government by representative assembly, and we vote mostly for personalities rather than issues. Those issues that reach public debate such as school bussing and abortion are superficial. Crucial issues like the banking and property laws seem to never surface. These laws are enacted with little fanfare and even less public debate. There may be extensive wrangling about how much spending on education will increase, but what we are going to do to get the best teachers at the earliest grade levels is never under discussion.

Part of my American heritage says that governments tend to become corrupt and the only thing that can keep the government honest is the vigilance and determination of the citizen himself. This is why we have trial by jury of peers, who are supposed to be fellow citizens, preferably those who know the person on trial. With a jury trial both the law and the facts of the case are considered by the jury. If the law is seen to be unjust or abusive the jury has the power to vote for acquittal. Judges and prosecutors generally will not tell jurors this, but read your American history and find out why we have a jury of peers. It is to prevent abuse of the law above all else, not simply to determine the facts of a case. People empowered with this knowledge can make a big difference. It is their only real chance to abolish unjust laws.

Speaking of laws, a general law of nature is that if a thing can happen it will. This is a rule that includes Murphy's Law. It seems to me that if I were an official in one or another government agency,

I could supplement my salary by doing favors for those in the know. Whether I worked for the FBI, IRS, OSHA, EPA, FDA, FmHA or whatever, I could use my bureaucratic powers to make life miserable and doing business nearly impossible for virtually any target I was commissioned to "get." By seizing assets and bank accounts, I would close down operations, declare equipment and procedures unsafe, confiscate inventories etc. From a representative of an industry threatened by an upstart innovator, to a wheeler dealer with a grudge to settle, anyone could let me know whom to go after and I would set my portion of government in motion to do the dirty deed.

Since this can happen (and undoubtedly does) the larger our bureaucracies the worse we can expect our government to be.

And then there is what may be called benign oversight. A few years ago I visited the home of a friend. Her father, in his shorts, was just putting away his home insect spraying outfit after completing his weekly spraying for bugs. I asked him if he wasn't concerned about spraying toxic chemicals in his house. "Oh no," he responded. "If it was dangerous the government wouldn't let them sell it." I shut up and said no more, but he may have been regrettably naive considering that four years later both he and his wife are dead from cancer. I believe it is unrealistic to place this kind of faith in government.

For my own part I have been uncomfortable with the term citizen since the Viet Nam war. So many people are on one side or the other, whether they supported the war or not, but from every viewpoint I can see, no matter which side you were on, our government betrayed its citizens. How can you feel you owe allegiance to a government like that? I am an American, but I don't have a sense of being a U.S. citizen. Though I cannot be more than an eighth Cherokee by blood, emotionally and philosophically I am all Indian in my commitment to survival on territory controlled by a hostile government. Not that anyone in the government would admit to being hostile, of course, since their hostility is covert.

I try to simply tolerate government, not to support it. I am convinced that there is a higher political consciousness that operates most of the time so that people treat each other with good taste, mutual respect and cooperation, or what passes for these in various quarters. Government, as far as I'm concerned, reminds me of exercising in a sweat suit with all kinds of weights strapped all over me. It is challenging exercise, but it is not something I think of as joyous.

It may not be easy to tap into this higher political awareness when government is all set up like some kind of machine, programed to carry on automatically, without further attention. Such government tends to roll over a few people here and grind up a few more there, and create more havoc than was ever intended. Those within it with a little awareness frequently exploit it to their own ends, and if someone receiving government attention does not keep his wits about him it could be pretty tough luck.

I am not a joiner of movements or a believer in formulas for dealing with government excesses. But most of my life I have been trying to learn when and how to stick up for myself and insist on the sort of polite society I want around me. I believe it is something I have to insist on too. It is not automatic just because of some constitution and a slew of laws.

In the following story I find it pretty hard to believe that the police officials were not engaged in securing revenue for their town by issuing traffic tickets. I do not believe highway safety was ever a real issue, although they claimed it was.

In the end I do not think it was the law that prevailed. Rather I think it was good sense, and that is the way it ought to be.

I might add that the reason we have a jury trial system is to see to it that when the law and good sense are in conflict, good sense prevails.

"Government is nine tenths bluff to begin with."

– Lou Murray

An Encounter With the Law

At 4:30 p.m. on Wednesday, January 20, 1993 I am traveling west on highway 314 near Benton, Tennessee. The speedometer does not work properly on the '79 Ford Courier pickup I'm driving, so I do not know my precise speed. Nevertheless, upon encountering a 45 mph sign I slack off from my already leisurely rate. Ordinarily I just keep up with traffic, but there is none in either direction, and no pedestrians.

The Speed Trap

At the top of the second little hill is a 35 mph sign, and I ease off the accelerator all the way so as to coast downhill. I'm ready to use the brake if there's any real need, and I keep a watchful eye out. A '79 Ford Courier has front disc brakes that're really superior, but the little Mazda engine doesn't have much pep. You learn to conserve momentum when you drive it.

Hidden over the top of the hill, just past the 35 mph sign, is a city police car in an empty church parking lot on the right hand side of the road. So, despite the unobstructed road conditions, I hit the brake to be sure I've complied with the law, regardless that it is probably written with old folks and hot rodders and rush hour traffic in mind.

I'm a conservative driver with 30 years experience, millions of miles, and a good driving record entering this rural town at an utterly tranquil hour. I don't have time to waste, but I'm in no hurry.

It's not much farther to the intersection with highway 411. After the next little rise, I give the gas a cautious foot so I'm certain I'm not exceeding their speed limit. However, the police car is right behind me with lights flashing. I get out and it's the police chief, Dennis Waters, with all his badges shining so bright I can hardly read them.

"What's the problem?" I ask.

He responds, "Did you know you were doing 51 in a 35 mph zone?"

"No sir." I answer truthfully. I could have maybe been doing 36 or something, but not 51 since the beginning of the zone. True it was a 45 zone just before that, and I just eased up a little from my highway pace which I don't know quite what that was with this speedometer. But, I wasn't in a hurry and wasn't driving unsafely. Was he going to stretch this into a ticket?

"Is there any reason you should be exceeding the speed limit?" he demands.

"No sir." I respond. Confound it, this is a 'have you stopped beating your wife' question. Whether I answer yes or no I acknowledge I was speeding, and I didn't exceed his speed limit. I slowed down a little extra upon passing him, waiting in his parking lot by the 35 sign.

But, I never argue with police officers, having heard too many stories of what can happen when one does, and I'm not one for violence.

What's the Hurry?

I stand around in circles in the empty intersection while he gets back in his car with my Georgia driver's license and all his gadgets, writing. He's in a hurry. Soon he hops out and pushes his ticket at me.

"Sign here!"

I don't think he's run my name through his computer, checked my registration or insurance, or anything else. He's getting his speeding ticket express style. I get the impression he wants to finish with me so he can get back to where he was hiding. There's not much traffic on this highway at this time of day, and maybe he wants to make the most of it.

"No sir." I rejoin. I don't like his hurry, I don't like his attitude, and I don't like his purpose.

I'd been alert, seen all the signs including him, and had responded reasonably under the circumstances. I never had a patrolman write a ticket so fast, but what do I know with my lifetime total of five speeding tickets? Sure, I'm out of state, vulnerable and don't have friends nearby. But I work hard for a living, while this guy lies in wait. Now he's in a rush to take my little money with his pen.

I have to really be in a hurry to push it on a two lane road, and I wasn't and hadn't, and let's take a breath here folks and be calm. I don't like being hustled into signing something I haven't read.

"Why not?" he says, apparently surprised.

"I'm not signing anything I don't understand," I say. At the least I want to see what his ticket is all about. I wasn't in a hurry before I saw him, and I'm sure not going to be now.

"What is it you don't understand?" he returns, exasperated.

It is just barely misting. Not enough for more than an occasional wiper pass over the windshield. "Get in the patrol car out of the rain," he offers, "and I'll explain it."

I tell him, "I saw the speed limit signs and you, and I didn't think I was speeding."

He shows me his radar, which has 51 on its digital readout. Maybe he clocked me doing this at the beginning of the 35 zone?

Many pundits say if you break the law you must pay, meaning if you violate the strictest, narrowest interpretation you are guilty. No appeal to common sense, no room for reason.

But, somehow the law has to be sensible.

Tightening the Screws

He explains further that he likes writing tickets least of all his duties, and if he just gave someone else a ticket for doing 50 in that zone he couldn't let me off for doing 51.

One thing I decide I should find out, so I ask, "What if I don't sign?"

"If you don't sign I'll have to arrest you, call a wrecker and have your truck towed in, and you'll have to post bond to get out of jail. Your signature is your bond. If you don't sign you'll have to put up a cash bond or go to jail."

Now my feathers are ruffled. I have heard of policemen in more serious cases than this giving people the respect and courtesy of following the arresting officer to the jail, parking and locking up their vehicle. At the least he could let me pull it off the road. I haven't tried to run from him and I'm not going to. It isn't even my truck. It's a friend's.

No cars come down 314 the whole fifteen minutes we are parked in the middle of the road. I take my time, considering my options.

Only a few blocks away from the county courthouse and his town hall, he's going to arrest me like a dangerous criminal and add who knows how much in towing and storage charges, plus the the terror that I can't lock up the truck so it'll be safe. It could be stripped, as is not uncommon in the police pounds in New Orleans near where I grew up. There the police tow away tourist cars for parking violations in the French Quarter, but they can't stop the thefts and vandalism in their impoundment lots. Under a veneer of propriety they are ravening wolves. I'd just been curious, but now I am glad I asked. The policeman is doing a marvelous job of explaining his ticket.

"Let me get my glasses so I can read this." Being far-sighted, I have a little blurring of detail close up, and I want to read his fine-print.

His ticket says the fine is not to exceed fifty dollars. But he has written on the ticket that bond is $82.50. How could they have a bond higher than the maximum for the offense? Court costs? I'm no lawyer and don't know how these things are figured, but it doesn't sound right to me. It just makes me more suspicious. I think all they really want is that easy money.

Sure enough the next thing he's telling me is if I pay the bond I won't have to show up in court. Could bond be some way to turn a maximum $50 offense into $82.50 or more on tickets issued to people from the city that want to be home on Monday evening traffic court night? Could be, but how to prove it? For sure you'd hear a thousand pounds of pious nonsense about being the guardians of highway safety for any shred of evidence that the revenue from such tickets greased the skids in Benton, Tennessee.

So, to avoid financial and mechanical disaster I sign his ticket, adding "without prejudice" to indicate I'm doing so as an expedient, not as validation.

Traffic Court

The court date is February 15, 7:00 p.m., a national holiday. Well, Benton isn't going to hold their traffic court on a national holiday are they?

Yes, they are, but I'm there. I don't trust them at any turn now.

I plead not guilty. Though I can't be certain of my exact speed when clocked, I was fresh, alert, aware of the speed zones, and had complied with them. Whatever the radar readout, I hadn't at any time violated the intent of the law.

I find, according to the officer's testimony, that I was clocked twice in rapid succession right at the beginning of the 35 zone, before Chief Waters left the parking lot or noticed me hitting my brakes. The way his equipment works, he never clocked me again because then he wouldn't have had the 51 reading on his machine.

I also find that when he asked me if I realized I'd been doing 51 in a 35 zone, and I responded, "No sir," he concluded I hadn't known it was a 35 zone. Maybe he catches a lot of people who don't see his sign, but for him to assert I was barreling along at 51 right on through his 35 zone was just plain false and wrong, and I wasn't going to agree. Regardless of minor technicality, I hadn't been driving unsafely, though I had never been to Benton before or known of the haste or rigor with which they administered their laws.

I saw their minds were made up. So, to indicate the soul searching of my defense and how I felt, I let them know they could do what they wanted. I wasn't prepared to pay their fine and would go to jail instead. Even then, I wanted a jury trial.

I am the first case. Real private. Just me, Chief Waters and Ms. Stevens, the magistrate, in her office. They send me back out to wait, as they're not sure what to do yet.

After everyone else is bundled through--and I have no idea of the other cases or their nature, as this seems to be a private rather than a public court--they call me back in.

A Fine Kettle of Fish

The magistrate has the police chief explain about time served in jail if you don't pay your fine. Get this.

I would get credit for $8 a day, time served. But they don't have their own jail and have to use the Polk County jail and that costs them $21.80 a day. So, they are going to charge me that and add it on to my fines. I will never get my fine paid off, just go deeper and deeper in debt to the town of Benton the longer I sit in jail!

I don't think they can get away with this as it's a clear case of enslavement, but they soberly assure me it's their agenda. Well, this really gets my dander up and I suggest they go ahead, and when I finally get my jury trial we'll see. I don't think that twelve flesh and blood Americans are going to unanimously ignore an injustice like this, regardless of whatever laws might be on the books. This is exactly what we have trial by a jury of peers to eliminate, ever since the days of King George III. Any reasonably clear-minded jury would see who was guilty and of what.

I don't give an inch, despite the fact they are bristling like porcupines and I'm getting caught up in it too. It feels like they enforce just those laws that suit them--maybe simply make up the laws as they go along. (What I don't know yet is that Benton has a reputation for roughing up dissidents, even killing some every now and then. I even heard that when one of the victims of law enforcement in this town won a settlement for damages from the sheriff's department, he was found dead with a bullet in his brain before he could collect. Probable murder, unsolved.)

I do know this much. If their intent is a safe highway, they had that without ever ticketing me. If they want to teach me a lesson to be quicker and more exact in my compliance with their law, they have run me through all the inconvenience and trauma of their procedures. If they want to rub a real liberal dose of salt in the wound, then a week in jail will be plenty expense, inconvenience and hazard to my health, but I'll go if I have to.

None of the above apply, though. Their bottom line is money. If I don't learn to pay their regular rates of highway robbery they'll go through some kind of paperwork with the Georgia authorities about my license, plus threaten me with a jail that ups the ante at least $13.80 a day. And, the magistrate keeps asking me if I don't have friends or relatives that can be contacted--as though she has a pretty good idea she isn't getting any money out of me, but maybe she can scare my friends or relatives into paying. Well, she seems to know her business, but I'm not giving ground either, and I never admit to having any friends or relatives anywhere.

"You've got ten days to appeal." They assure me.

It turns out I can't appeal then and there, however, because it's a holiday and after hours, and they can't even put me in jail. Apparently they've tried to contact the sheriff, but can't reach him. If I want to appeal I have to come back again at whatever additional inconvenience. Not only that, according to them if I want to appeal I'll have to pay a $250 appeal bond. More court costs?

At this point her honor finds me guilty. She doesn't say what the fine is, and I precede them out of their office.

Don't Railroad Me without a Jury

I can't knuckle under to such a mish-mash of injustice. It isn't right, and something is moldering in Benton. If we let ourselves be ruled by the letter of the law to the exclusion of good sense we'll have a tyrannical and neurotic society in which people will fear and loathe the police and even their fellow citizens. I'm afraid this is what we do have, and it's suddenly my responsibility to see we *don't* have it, and I hope the jury will see I succeed.

So on Thursday, February 25, I appear at the Polk County courthouse in Benton to file my appeal. They are closed. It snowed all morning, and anyway, in Benton, I find to my surprise, they close up at noon on Thursdays. So I drop a letter in the mail indicating I was there and will return the next day.

When I get there the next morning Connie, the clerk of court, has my letter, and sure enough she confirms the practice of charging $21.80 room and board for each day spent in jail. And, they are not going to let me file an appeal unless I put up a property or cash bond for $250. I want her to put this in writing, but, of course, she demurs. A local judge, who happens to be present, concurs that these are the rules and adds kind of philosophically that the traffic courts have more power than the communist party in the '50s in Russia. They are plainly all old friends.

"What if I can't post bond? If I can't pay the ticket I sure can't put up a $250 bond."

"We can't help you." the clerk says, and in an aside to the judge, "I'm not going to listen to any more of this."

I stay a while longer looking at the cartoons on the wall, trying to get a feel for what is going on, and wondering what to do next. It's pretty tense. The clerk asks if I am waiting for someone. I respond that I'm thinking, but one of the things I can't help thinking is maybe they're afraid I *am* waiting for someone.

So, I ask her where I can find the district attorney. She offers to give me his address in Cleveland, Tennessee. It's the 10th judicial circuit and takes in four counties. Right as I'm copying down the address, the police chief and a sheriff's deputy come in and deploy behind the counters, keeping an eye on me. Maybe someone has called them to come deal with trouble. They try not to be too obvious about it, but they don't seem to have anything else on their agenda except watching me. I figure they are looking for some excuse to pounce, but outside of briefly locking eyes with Chief Waters, I'm careful not to give them any. The clerk has a phone call as I'm copying, and she is on the phone a long time. Despite the extremely edgy atmosphere, I wait until she is free again, thank her politely for her help, and leave.

Paranoia Plus

I get to the district attorney's office at 12:15 and everyone is out to lunch. About 1:15 one of the receptionists returns, and by 1:30 an assistant DA is in. She is briefly visible behind the thick plate glass at reception, and assures me she'll be available shortly. In a few more minutes two men in casual clothes enter. She lets them in and calls that she is ready for me.

"These two gentlemen are police officers." she says, indicating the couch behind me for them and arranging a chair off to the side of her desk for me. I imagine they have guns, as she is positioning herself well out of the line of fire. I wonder why she thinks she needs two police officers, but remembering the heavy plate glass at reception I suppose paranoia must be standard procedure in east Tennessee. Anyway, I greet them, turn my back and ignore them, and explain my problem.

164   *A Biodynamic Farm*

She listens to how I was threatened with perpetual jail for a traffic offense by way of charging me rent on my jail cell, and she indicates such rents are standard practice. I tell her about being denied an appeal because I couldn't put up an appeal bond, and she acknowledges this too is normal, and "What did I want from her?"

"I want to know how they can do a thing like this, and I want to see the statutes."

Maybe this is the right question, because instead of showing me the statutes she smiles and whips out a sheet of paper saying, "Here's what you need," and writes, "This man needs to fill out: *In forma pauperis*. February 26, 1993. Please allow Hugh Lovel to file an appeal bond on his speeding charge. Thanks, Sarah."

Then she gives me what must be a standard challenge in her line of work, "But, if you appeal you will lose!" and I get the impression that she'll probably be the one prosecuting the case.

Maybe my face betrays I don't think I'll lose. I would rather have her underestimate me. But, she suddenly has a better idea, and writes at the top of the page, "Is it possible to reduce the fine to $5." She doesn't use a question mark, as if to emphasize she's giving directions.

"Have them contact whoever issued the ticket and see if they can reduce the fine so you can pay it. Do that first." she says, and accents this by numbering her second idea (1) and the *In forma pauperis* (2). "Give this to them." she smiles, "They'll recognize my handwriting."

As I get up to leave she admonishes me not to speed any more, while I assure her I was not speeding. "I believe you," she confides. This is the first hint of anything honestly human I've seen in the whole mess so far.

Sidestepping Provocation

I get back to the clerk of court's office and hand Connie the paper. She doesn't know what to do, but she gets the bond form. Right there on the form is the *In forma pauperis* part for those who haven't the money to post bond. Clearly they would never have told me.

"You realize your ticket's going to cost you more if you appeal it." the clerk proceeds.

"That's not the way I understood it in the DA's office." I assure her.

"Well, it will." she asserts.

By this time Chief Waters and the sheriff's deputy file back in and take up their posts. Along with them come two aggressive looking men in plain clothes who walk right in behind the counters like they own the place. I can't help but wonder what these people are so afraid of. This is a traffic offense and they act like they are preparing to beat up Rodney King. Do police have this sort of attitude across the country?

The clerk discovers at this point that the *In forma pauperis* procedure includes the words "resident of the state of Tennessee" and she says, "But you say you're a resident of Georgia."

"I don't have any trouble with that." I assure her. "I can strike through Tennessee and write in Georgia. It's not like I won't appear. I will appear."

"Well, I don't know." she says. "I'll have to call her."

She gets on the phone to Sarah, while the more aggressive of the two men in street clothes thrusts himself up to the counter with, "You've got a problem."

It's not a question. It's a statement meant to provoke me, and he's all pumped up with his chin out. But I'm having none of it. I tell him, "She's taking care of it," and ignore him until he subsides again. I can see that at the least misstep all four of these "officers of the law" will jump me, beat me to a pulp, maybe kill me. They reek with fear and aggression. But, I had years of walking bridge beams high off the ground, carrying tools and construction materials. I fear heights and know what they can do, but I won't be distracted from my purpose.

The clerk of court, still on the phone, tells me "We can't do your bond. You'll have to do it in Georgia." and, "Here. I'll let you talk to her."

She gives me the phone, and Sarah tells me I'll have to file my *In forma pauperis* in Georgia, there's no way I can do it in Tennessee. And, what was I doing going to her for help anyway? She was the opposition!

She doesn't know, of course, that I don't usually navigate by logic. As a farmer I prefer to do it by feel. "I know that." I tell her, "But, somehow, I had the sense I'd get a little fair play."

"Well, I've given you that," she says. "But didn't you see if they'd reduce the fine first?"

"I went back to the clerk's office and showed her your message."

"Well, have her call the town magistrate and see if they'll reduce the fine."

Backing Down in Confusion

I give the clerk the phone back and tell her the lady DA wants her to call the town magistrate to see if she'll reduce the fine, but I think it will make a better impression if I go over there and bring Sarah's note first hand. And, thanks very kindly for all her help.

I leave briskly and precede my police honor guard to the town hall, a block away. I'm walking and more mobile than they are with their cars.

I see the magistrate, show her the note from Sarah, and she is studying it as Chief Waters and his provocateur plainclothesman file into her office. These people are all scared, and I can see it in the way they stare, lick their lips and swallow as if their mouths are dry.

The magistrate ventures, "Well, I don't think the fine is but $2 anyway."

"The ticket says it cannot exceed $50." I point out.

"It's $82.50," bursts the police chief. "Well, the fine's $13.50 and the rest's court costs."

I see they're in confusion. What have they been doing all this time about fines and court costs? Chief Waters pulls a large book down off the shelf like he's going to look up something. He did this previously when trying to decide how much credit I'd get for jail time, and I have to wonder what's in this book. It doesn't look like anything they are going to let me see, since Ms. Stevens asks me to wait outside. She's going to have to call Sarah.

It takes a while for them to make up their minds what to do, but when I'm called in again the magistrate starts off with, "The way this ticket has been handled is highly irregular."

"Personally I wish he'd appeal." the police chief says.

"I do too." I assure him. He probably figures he can sway the jurors because, being local, they'll have to live with the threat of him thereafter. But he doesn't realize the first thing I'd have to do once my appeal is registered is petition for a change of venue. No way I'd get a fair trial in his town.

"Well, we're going to drop the fine," allows the magistrate, "But you realize you're still guilty. I mean, we found you guilty," she fumbles.

"Sarah's got a soft heart," allows the police chief, as though if it was up to him he'd go ahead and ride roughshod over people.

I don't say anything for a minute. I can't help but think that Sarah's the only one of them with a lick of sense. But the situation seems to require some kind of an acknowledgement. So, I tell the magistrate, "I heard you." I realize she needs some way to save face and pretend I agreed with her.

On the Road Again

She stares at me some more, and kind of as an afterthought says, "I thought you felt this was an injustice."

"I do. I do think it's an injustice." I rejoin.

But, that seems to be the end of it. She knows and I know that if I can't support their speeding racket in the first place I'm not going to pursue an appeal either, even if it is *In forma pauperis*. I've already spent nearly forty dollars driving back and forth to their town on this matter, and how will I recover that or compensation for my time spent on it? Sue them after I win a jury trial? And maybe if I won damages they could still appeal? Besides, having anything to do with them may be deadly.

I ask if that is all, and may I go? She nods. I ask her for Sarah's note back and leave.

Chapter XIV

In the proceeding two chapters I presented concepts that may be useful in developing an awareness of the threefold social order and its economic, political and significance spheres. In the process I had to grapple with terminology to name the significance sphere. Some have called it the religious/cultural sphere, but I believe this has led to misunderstandings. It must be clear that science, religion, philosophy, art and all aesthetic endeavors are included. Insofar as this sphere is good--that is, liberative and enabling--it deals with truth and values.

These three divisions of society parallel the human individual's head, heart and guts, and thought, emotion and will. The economic sphere relates to substance, mass, physical reality and its resources and limitations. This is the guts of society and determines the character of the social will. The political sphere corresponds to the heart, as it reflects a society's emotional milieu. It stands in the middle, mediating between the concrete economic sphere and its opposite polarity of significance.

Everything massive, no matter how great or minute, has accompanying significance. On the grand scale we attach significance to the various planetary masses and their motions relative to each other and the celestial background. Without mass we have nothing on which to pin significance, while without significance the existence of mass is questionable.

The artist, musician, writer succeed insofar as they convey something of significance. Likewise the scientist, philosopher, religionist all strive for significance regardless of their ways and means.

As indicated in the introduction to chapter one, I became a farmer out of a quest for significance. When I entered college I intended to major in music. However, during registration I was working, so my mother signed me up in the business curriculum, perhaps thinking to get me involved in something practical. Inertia kept me from righting this, until after a few days of classes I became intrigued by what was being taught in my business courses. It took me a year and a half to become disillusioned by what I learned about our economic system.

I changed my major to sociology thinking of becoming a priest. But, within another year I was disaffected with a ministry that I felt claimed to have all the answers--except the answer to why was the need for ministry always growing.

It is not much help to a starving man to make him dependent on the breadlines. He benefits more from a few fishhooks and some seed corn. Likewise the priesthood might do more than dole out a meager spiritual reassurance. It should lead people to find truth, hope and empowerment where these things originate in personal everyday life.

I became so embarrassed by the inspirational poverty of people proclaiming themselves Christians that I gave up on the priesthood and joined the military to fight Communism. Inevitably this too was disillusioning, and I turned to the study of biochemistry, thinking this was where I would really find out about life. But even the best chemists were in the dark about life, and I turned to LSD and studying Tibetan Buddhism. Although in some ways this too was unconstructive, at least I had turned my quest for significance inward to unravel the puzzle of me and make sense out of my existence.

By a series of improbable events I met Jack Horner, an actor, writer, philosopher, lecturer, and above all explorer of human nature. In the 50s and 60s, along with such pioneers as L. Ron Hubbard, John McMasters, Charlie Broaded and Donald Kingsbury, he helped develop a new approach to therapy which acknowledged that though people certainly had bodies, they were not merely their bodies.

As a gift of profound caring, Jack passed on what he could of the fruits of his investigations to the few hundred people he trained in his school of eductive psychology, the Personal Creative Freedoms Foundation. He is gone now, and as far as I know nothing remains of his school. His graduates are dispersed. Many like myself no longer work directly in the field of psychology.

Nonetheless, I owe him a large debt and consider it worthwhile to pass on in this book some of what I gained in my association with him. It is of significant cultural value and has been of incalculable benefit in establishing a biodynamic farm.

"I am afraid the difference in education which people can get is very wide. And I'm also afraid that at this time the education which is given in grade school, high school and the university is very thoroughly destructive toward the initiative and ability of human beings."

-L. Ron Hubbard

Something to Think About

Although a brilliant lecturer and incisive writer, Jack Horner was not a psychology teacher in the sense of someone who holds forth information and expects it to be memorized. He wanted his students to realize and make discoveries as a result of their own spiritual and mental endeavors. In this way he awakened skills and knowledge that people knew were their own, not taken on faith.

Basic Exercises

Jack started his students out with certain basic exercises. Each drill built on the one before it so the development of skills was cumulative. The fundamental drill was one of intent, open-minded observation. He called this basic exercise 0.

Helping clients delve into their psyches and sort out the gaps, confusions and conflicts required focusing attention in an attentive, yet non-judgmental way. The idea was to make it safe to dramatize virtually anything no matter how stupid or nutty it might seem. Invalidation, evaluation or advice had to be avoided as they ruined therapy.

Open-minded, intent observation paved the way for acknowledgement. The second drill, basic exercise 1, was one of completing cycles by acknowledgement. When asking questions or giving instructions it was important to complete each cycle by acknowledging the answer or response. Being unbiased was key since passing judgment, agreeing, disagreeing, approving or disapproving all interfered with completing the cycle.

The third drill, basic exercise 2, was one of follow through. Asking questions or giving instructions needed to get all the responses, not just one. This frequently meant repeating a question or instruction many times, always as though it was the first time.

Resolving mental and emotional turmoil required non-judgmental observation and acknowledgment all along the way. But, to examine any issue properly meant looking at it from a variety of viewpoints. If problems were seen in sufficient perspective they resolved, and all the psychologist did was direct the client's attention to the problem area.

Although this basic skill is useful under any circumstances, it is especially helpful to the psychologist/client relationship. Usually one round of questions or instructions just scratches the surface of a client's associated mental and emotional material. As long as a set of questions or instructions is productive of change it should be delivered over again as though it is completely new. This way all avenues are explored including those obscured by confusion and counter-intention.

These are all fundamental skills that mothers should foster in children right from the start, long before they learn the alphabet or numbers.

The GSR and Repetitive Processes

As an adjunct to eductive processes Jack trained us to use a galvanic skin response meter. This helped tell whether a set of questions or instructions was appropriate and producing change or not. It also helped prevent impatience and prejudice from influencing therapy. As long as the meter showed charge we gave the same series of questions or instructions over and over again.

Such a process might involve, "Tell me something you are willing to talk to me about." Inevitably the client will think of things he is unwilling to talk about. But, whatever his answer, it is acknowledged with "okay", "all right", "good", "fine" or "thank you." The next question is, "Tell me something about that." This answer is also acknowledged and it is back to, "Tell me something you are willing to talk to me about." Then again, "Tell me something about that." These two instructions are cycled through hundreds or even thousands of times.

This is a fundamental repetitive process that pretty much assures the client will look repeatedly at all the things he fears he never can talk to anyone about. It is especially effective if one gets the client to divide his life up into periods which can be cycled through asking specifically about each in turn. Suppressed or invalidated material often comes up from these periods.

For instance, the question might be, "From birth to kindergarten (or first grade) tell me something you are willing to talk to me about." Then the next round might be, "During elementary school. . ." and the next, "During middle school. . ." and so on.

At the beginning the galvanic skin response meter registers signs of emotional stress as the client considers talking about touchy subjects. It may be hard work coming up with safe topics. Eventually after completion of cycle after cycle with only open-minded, attentive, non-judgmental acknowledgement in return the client will try out the taboo topics. The biofeedback device registers the release of emotional charge but the client still gets the same acknowledgement each complete cycle. By the time the GSR meter registers no further emotional charge the client has discovered the freedom of talking about what previously were some pretty touchy subjects.

Freedom Flows

It may be advisable at this point to ask the client a few rounds of, "Tell me something you are free to talk to me about," and, "Tell me something you are free not to talk to me about," eliciting the freedom to either talk about a subject or not talk about it, whichever is appropriate.

There are various ways of repeating a line of questioning too. It need not all be cyclical repetition of a small set of questions. One example, creative definition procedure, (included as an appendix) is a set of eighteen questions designed to examine the definitions of a word or symbol from a variety of viewpoints. For the eductive psychologist, this is especially useful, since it may make many lines of questioning more meaningful for the client.

Collapsed Concepts

One of the commonest problems we face communicating with ourselves and others is having the definitions of two or more words collapsed. For instance many people think that discipline means punishment, problem means overwhelm, learn means parrot, occult means demonic, love means sex, or wealth means money. This sort of thing hampers thinking and can be severely disabling. Sometimes running words like help, problem or control through creative definition procedure can lead to astonishing results, clearing up a great deal of confusion.

What You Seek You Find

The universe has an amazing ability to conform to our thinking. One way of expressing this is Jesus' teaching that what we seek we will find. Frequently people do not realize this is a double edged sword. We may seek a thing either out of desire or aversion. What we seek to resist and avoid will be what we find, fully as much as what we seek to become or attain.

For instance, the US government in its avowed resistance to the tyranny and oppression of fascism and communism has become an oppressive government itself, especially in regard to victimless crimes. An example of this is the "war on drugs" with its crude emotional propaganda aimed at racial and cultural minorities-- while it condones the most lucrative drug trade of all, prescription drugs. We are no more going about creating a drug free society than pigs fly. On the whole we are creating a drug dependent society despite various efforts to substitute nutritious, wholesome food for drugs. Needless to say, turning to nutritious food would obviate the police state nonsense about fighting drugs while we become increasingly dependent upon them.

Finding Freedom

There is no way in such a brief presentation as this to cover all the territory Jack's investigations spanned. Basically, working with body language and biofeedback (particularly the galvanic skin response) he found it easy to tell what increased freedom and ability for an individual. Bodily resistance rose as emotional conflicts clouded thinking. Invalidation, suppression and misidentification only added to that resistance.

On the other hand, clear, incisive thought with a high degree of reality decreased resistance. In order to increase a client's freedom and ability one got the client to examine an area of high resistance. By skillfully directing the client's attention, a little at a time, an increase of clarity, reality and correct identification resulted along with decreased resistance.

The changes thoughts cause in the galvanic skin response are so instantaneous and marked they can be easily observed. This means that out of the trillions of possible answers to a question, if one thought shows a high degree of reality for the client he can be directed to pick that thought out from the many as a valid answer. In this way lines of investigation can be pursued willingly by clients at a level of reality that otherwise might be impossible.

Biofeedback and Personal Reality

Biofeedback can be used to help people recall intricate details of incidents previously inaccessible to conscious memory. Birth and death experiences frequently are the most charged. It does not help that many are unwilling to accept the reality of recalling either a birth or a death experience. Accordingly, these incidents build up invalidation, suppression and misidentification. Clearly if the galvanic skin response shows the experience is real, it is real. Learning not to quibble with that is itself mind expanding.

Many things that are really real for people go beyond the bounds of modern scientific belief and its materialistic epistemology. People have reality on such things as being possessed by entities, having lived past lives, talking to the dead, out of body experiences, reading other people's minds, encountering extraterrestrials, choosing their birth into this life and learning lessons or carrying goals over from previous lifetimes.

Carl Sagan might ridicule the idea of aliens among us and argue that if we had extraterrestrials around we would have picked up their radio signals--as if extraterrestrials had no choice but to use radio to communicate. Nonetheless for many people extraterrestrials are real. Likewise materialistic science, not knowing any explanation for discarnate entities, memories of past lifetimes, out of body experiences, etc., invalidates them as fantasy. Biofeedback shows the most effective approach is to accept these things with an open mind and acknowledge them as real.

Ideality

To greater or lesser degrees everyone has the experience of finding the world does not conform to what he imagines as ideal. Usually this experience is rooted very early in life. Births often are difficult. They may involve stress in coming from darkness into bright light, from a warm fluid environment into cool air, anesthetics and other drugs, rough handling, etc. Any or all of these may serve to establish the belief that the world is far from ideal.

Of course, there is no guarantee what any given person's reaction will be. One person upon seeing a red ball is attracted to it, while another is annoyed. Upon seeing a dog one infant may shriek in terror while another responds with interest and affinity.

There is reason to believe we share common archetypal standards, though we each see these from different viewpoints and form different opinions. There is a tendency to think of one's own view as right and others' views as wrong or invalid, and one might go to considerable lengths to prove his view correct. As a means for overcoming invalidation proving self correct frequently is unfortunate since inevitably it leads to further invalidations.

Prejudices compound themselves and individuals develop intricate, automatic, unthinking ways of solving the problems of life in a non-ideal world. For one thing, past efforts to cope may have been so painful and embarrassing one does not want to think about them any more. On the occasions when one or more of these systems fail, there is further invalidation, leading to further problems with a stubbornly non-ideal world.

By the time people reach adulthood their development is so channeled that only modest rehabilitation can be accomplished, even with the most skilled therapy. Human beings have untold creative powers, but for most these fall short of realization.

Better than Therapy

In general there is more that can be accomplished by improved rearing of children than by therapy of the already disabled. This is not to say therapy is useless. But simple home birth in relatively dim light and warm water tends to minimize the child's initial invalidation of the world. Nor can breast feeding be ignored, as mother's milk is the ideal food. Substitutes again may evoke the notion that the world cannot match one's ideals.

In the first few hours, days and weeks the patterns of behavior of later life become established. By the time a person learns to talk, basic reaction patterns, such as forcing people to pay attention, or conversely, ignoring them, are set behaviors. Moreover these reactions are multiple, complex and form different patterns for each individual.

Then there is early schooling. Much of what passes for elementary education again tends to invalidate what is perceived as ideal, so home schooling with its intensive individual attention (and without invalidation, evaluation and advice) is preferable.

Nothing, however, is so early and so basic to individual development as nutrition. Learning to grow food that builds a better bridge between the will and the imagination is the kind of thinking that leads to better thinking.

Garlic harvest time at Union Agricultural Institute, Blairsville, Georgia. Garlic is one of more than a hundred different crops raised on this biodynamic farm.

Chapter XV

As the end of the century comes, several things must be faced. The food supply is not only tainted, it is devitalized. Especially, foods lack nourishment for integrity, uprightness and willingness. These qualities may depend upon individual attitudes, but they require nutritional support.

We live in a poorly integrated society that says one thing but does another. The war on Communism claimed to be protecting our freedom and our assets, but it was used to rationalize tyranny and environmental destruction. The war on poverty claimed it would eliminate the beggar on the streets, but it institutionalized dependency in an even bigger way. The war on drugs more than anything seems to be an excuse to abolish civil liberties. And, we are preparing for educational and health care crusades that will no more address the roots of these problems than whales will fly. The role of the U.S. presidency appears to be basically more and more of the same, just marketed differently by different administrations.

Perhaps more significantly, on the economic scene we face the imminent collapse of our financial institutions, many of which are holding companies, perhaps set up for bankruptcy court. International depositors (many of them Japanese and Arabic?) could be left in the cold. When a bank goes bankrupt is it not the depositors who lose? How will they take this? Moreover, capital is withdrawing from America to buy assets in Russia and eastern Europe following the Iron Curtain's collapse while real aid to these people has been tenuous, perhaps to convince them to sell cheap.

Americans assumed their salaries, wages, promotions and retirement programs were on a schedule, fixed and assured. This has left many drowning in debt while bankruptcies, reorganizations, takeovers and imports from low wage countries change the rosy picture. Despite low mortgage rates, real estate prices have faltered, not just for farms and small town dwellings, but for homes in and near major cities. The savings and loan crisis is affecting banks. The nation's largest employers keep laying off workers. Pension funds have lost large sums in junk bonds. Perhaps most ominous of all, the US Government owes trillions, and as guarantor of deposits in banks and savings and loans this could go many times higher. Yet, one area we definitely are not cutting back on is police. *The US has more laws, lawyers, police, judges, crimes, and people behind bars per capita of any country, including, as far as I can tell, such trouble spots as Russia, South Africa, Israel and China.*

Most Americans can read, but they prefer the ease of watching videos. This goes hand in hand with Americans being the most overfed and undernourished people on earth. We know there is a hidden epidemic of AIDS, but that may not be half of it. Officially there is little to worry about, and just stick with the programming. But, how long will it be before borders are closed to all but specially authorized traffic?

Things could get worse, and probably they will before they get better. On the one hand it could be said that we face slavery and ruin due to our own hypocrisy and moral poverty.

On the other hand the handwriting is on the wall for those inclined to see. More and more people are taking responsibility for their own lives by way of home birthing, breast feeding, home schooling, alternative medical therapies, a wellness approach to health, recycling, edible landscaping and building energy efficient, non-toxic homes.

In terms of fitting my farm venture into this picture, a CSA co-op was a natural development.

"I guess I'm not what you call 'politically minded.' I don't much care how they run it--except, well, there ought to be a sort of looseness about it. You know--a man ought to be able to do what he wants to, if he can, and not be pushed around."

--Robert Heinlein

Community Sponsored Agriculture

Here and there people are looking at their options and choosing to make a difference. They want to support endeavors that remedy the problems caused by the bigger-is-better mindset. One of the worst concerns is the loss of more than seventy percent of the world's topsoil in the last hundred and fifty years. Instinctively people sense a need to encourage sound agriculture. At the same time they want to buy food that not only is free of pollution, but has an inner, vital impulse toward life. These and related factors motivate a trend toward agriculturally based producer/consumer communities that regenerate the land which feeds them.

Forming a CSA

The acronym, CSA, stands for Consumer Supported Agriculture, Community Sponsored Agriculture, or Community Supported Agriculture, depending on who is using it. In all cases it indicates a vertically integrated agricultural operation.

However it may be done, the CSA group provides what is necessary to grow their food. Fortunately, not everyone has the same things to contribute. Usually farmers who can work the land successfully are in the shortest supply. But, from these farmers' points of view, consumers are in short supply or laborers are hard to find at crucial times. The CSA is not functional until farmer, farmland, labor, operating capital and consumers are lined up in cooperation.

CSA farms vary. Some are located in or near metropolitan areas where consumer interest is high. Others involve more distance between the land and consumers. Many sell "shares" in advance of their year's production. Others require an advance deposit, refundable in everything from produce, canned goods, eggs, honey and cheese, to meat, flowers, herbs, firewood or wool. In some cases consumers come to the farm to get their food. In others weekly deliveries to distribution points may be necessary. One CSA may have monthly potluck dinners, developing strong core groups and dividing up tasks between mothers, accountants, farm apprentices, lawyers, fixers and farmers, while others may be seat-of-the-pants operations stripped to the bare essentials.

CSAs have several things in common. In one way or another they all encourage farmers and consumers to understand and support each other. They enable participants to invest their resources in the land and its betterment. In a sense the means of production belongs to both producers and consumers, as they contribute skill, labor and capital, and take responsibility for leaving the land better off for their use of it. Nevertheless, in some cases the land is owned privately, while in others the CSA is organized as a co-operative, a land trust or a research and training institute.

Benefits

Besides nutritious food and a healthier environment there are many subsidiary benefits. By having the moral and financial support of a community, the farmer has backing for experimentation. Members may want exotic items like Chinese cabbage, Armenian cucumbers, Roquefort cheese or Louisiana hot sauce, and the farmer has to learn how to produce these things.

The CSA can also be an educational opportunity for young adults interested in becoming farmers. By apprenticing on a CSA farm they experience growing and preparing a wide variety of products. Moreover, members and their children learn how their food is produced, and there are therapeutic benefits in this especially for those growing or convalescing. Lastly, the farm is a haven from the vicissitudes of city life. Conceivably it will provide alternatives to employment in economic hard times.

The idea is that consumers support the farm and the farm supports consumers.

An Example

Since the only CSA I can really describe is the one I founded, I should briefly review how it developed.

During the '80s I endeavored to establish a functional fourteen acre biodynamic farm, Union Agricultural Institute, working off the farm to pay expenses. In '85 I was laid off as a bridge carpenter in Atlanta. In '86 and '87 I farmed full time, selling produce to stores and in parking lots. It was hardly a way to make ends meet. I knew there had to be a better way. The Biodynamic Association quarterly, *Biodynamics* ran an article on CSAs. I drew up a prospectus with a copy of the article and distributed it to a few people in the Atlanta area. They told friends, and I gave a couple of organizational lectures, showing slides, cow horns, my prep stirring and spraying equipment, and a few other farm tools such as the wheel hoe, the scuffle hoe and my scythe. For the first season I had twenty-eight members sign up.

I did not want to promise too much, so I offered only breads, honey, pollen, eggs, yogurt and vegetables in season. I asked for hundred dollar deposits, refundable in groceries. This money got me through February, March and April when I planted but had nothing to sell.

At the end of April I delivered my first orders of spinach, lettuce and seasonal herbs. The season progressed with green onions, garlic, English peas, sugar snap peas, yellow onions, potatoes, cabbage, parsley, snap beans, corn, summer squash, tomatoes, okra, beets, collards, leeks, winter squash, turnips and Chinese radishes. The garden was finished by mid November, though I made one last delivery after Thanksgiving for pork.

The farm was 125 miles from Atlanta, so I made a Saturday run to three drop-off points. Members received a weekly newsletter and order form that took two hours a week at the typewriter and copy machine. Bookkeeping was on index cards with names, addresses, dates and sums. Mostly I concentrated on running the farm, picking the number one veggies, recycling the residual vegetation through forty chickens, twenty rabbits and two pigs for fertilizer, and replanting with the next crop in the rotation. Although I kept bees, the honey and the raw milk for yogurt came from nearby farms. I bought organically grown wheat and rye for baking bread.

Out of twenty six weekly deliveries, I counted on members to order half the time with average orders of twenty dollars--a gross of $7,280. I believe I took in a little more than that, say $7,500 in round figures. I realize this may not seem like much, but my expenses were low enough to make ends meet. All I had was the land and a small pickup truck, rototiller, lawnmower, scythe, pitchfork, axe, scuffle hoe, claw cultivator, wheel hoe, push planter and seeds bred for response to my methods.

Expanding

Consumer interest was strong simply from word of mouth. I could expand, but a larger investment was required. The farm needed woodlots, barns, fences, greenhouses, pastures, orchards, fish ponds and fields all in good measure, none at the expense of the others. There was no hurry. The land was mixed forest slopes and bottomland with good water but not especially good sun. There was plenty of brush clearing, rock picking and hay planting to do, but only three or four acres could be added to the truck garden regardless of how much help and machinery I had.

At my organizational meetings in February and March of '89 I asked for a thirty three dollar membership fee as a capital investment in the farm, plus the hundred dollar deposit. Again bookkeeping only showed how much was paid and how much was delivered. I changed picking and baking to Saturdays, and packing and delivering to Sundays. This allowed members to visit the farm and participate in picking on weekends, while I caught the least city traffic on Sundays.

An apprentice, Matthew Persico, cut intensive beds into three acres of sod with the rototiller. We used the pig compost on a fourth of it, planting this in potatoes. In the rest we interplanted corn with soybeans as a cover crop to be followed by rye with vetch. We built a small barn with three stalls, hay storage and an apprentice's apartment. I bought two calves to raise in the small barn yard, and phased out the rabbits since cows made more compost and were easier to feed on a larger scale.

For fertilizer I bought hay, corn and soy meal for the animals while I cleared small pastures, orchards and hay fields. My intent was to achieve self-sufficiency, with the farm producing its own feeds, seeds and transplants, breeding its own livestock and producing its own compost.

Starting its sixth year in 1993, this CSA, UAI Co-op, is servicing over 100 households. We have a reconditioned 35-year-old tractor, a couple of apprentices, six acres of row crops, a milk cow, cheese, yogurt and butter making, three calves, two nearly grown beef animals, eighty chickens, two pigs and a wintertime firewood operation.

Outside of the soil it is not a capital intensive operation, despite an estimated $26,000 gross for 1993. Less than five percent of what grows on the farm is exported. The most important parts of the operation are timing, balance and momentum.

Following the Seasons

Peas must be planted as early as possible. In Union County Georgia we start in late February or early March. Lettuce, spinach and onions follow in early March. Although cabbage and collards can be direct seeded fairly early, I prefer to plant them under a row covering for transplanting when it warms up. Early plantings tend to get ahead of weeds better, though frequent cultivation, weather permitting, is advisable. Having permanent sod around all the cultivated beds helps considerably.

In winter and early spring the cows eat hay in the barn, and every so often it can be mucked out to make compost piles. With spring warmth the rye and clover covers on the beds shoot up and are cut for fresh feed or for hay. The stubble is sprayed with BD preps and cultivated two or three times over a three week period so that it is digested and mellow before planting.

Since my beds are level with my grassy borders, both can be mowed (simultaneously after crops are picked) to feed the cows, pigs or chickens. In May there is so much to cut that haystacks must be made, to be fed in the winter when all the corn stover is gone.

I set out my cabbages and potatoes in April, following with corn, beans and cucurbits in May, and tomatoes, peppers and okra in early June. Garlic is planted early the preceding October. I harvest it and yellow onions in June, and follow them with bush beans. As much as possible I stagger crops like spinach, lettuce, corn and beans to produce a moderate but steady flow, extending the season. I always put compost on greens, while root crops like carrots, radishes and turnips do much better following behind without compost.

Generally crops tend to follow the seasons. Spring is the season for the best greens, such as lettuces, spinach, mustards and green onions. Spring tapers off into summer with cabbages and collards. Summer is for fruits like squashes and melons, tomatoes and peppers, corn and beans. Fall is the best time of the year for root crops, turnips, carrots, winter radishes, beets and daikons.

During the growing season the chickens are fenced in a long, hillside coop containing a thick stand of bamboo and a nesting house. At the top of the chicken coop I add sawmill bark, sprinkled with dust from the local granite quarry, for bedding. My lawnmower has a rear bagging feature, and every day I give the chickens a heaping wheelbarrow load of grass, clover and herb clippings from around the beds, which I mow on a monthly schedule. This keeps the egg yolks yellow while adding to the deep litter in the coop. Every so often this is made into a compost pile.

I use a biodynamic planting calendar for working crops according to their root, fruit, flower or leaf characteristics. For example, while potatoes are actually a swollen stem formation, they are planted as though they were roots because the root-like characteristic is being emphasized. Likewise, cauliflower and broccoli, despite their being flowers, are planted as leaf crops because they have to be held back to the leafy stage of development. They are eaten only as buds, not flowers.

And I grow a lot of things for the overall balance and health of the farm although they do not directly produce income. Certain things, like planting the whole farm in cucumbers or selling off all the compost, I would never do.

Rotations and Interplanting

One of the goals of crop rotation is to allow for a healthy nitrogen cycle while cropping. Compost is given liberally to leafy crops that need plenty of nitrogen, such as lettuce, spinach, cabbage and collards. It may be given more sparingly to fruiting crops which follow the greens, such as corn, squash, tomatoes and okra. It is withheld entirely from the root crops, such as carrots, radishes and turnips, which follow the fruits. I tend to lime legumes such as beans, peas and vetch which follow the roots, drawing in new nitrogen and producing rich compost as farm animals digest the vines. Then the cycle begins again with compost to the greens.

Another goal of crop rotation is to vary as much as possible the types of plants grown. Thus I follow lettuce with carrots, or collards with onions, but I never follow lettuce with spinach or carrots with parsnips.

There is also interplanting. Corn can be planted with soybeans, garlic with winter spinach, tomatoes with sweet basil, dill with cabbages and cukes, summer squash with popcorn, pumpkins with field corn, winter rye with rape, mustard, turnips and vetch. This encourages abundance by fitting more species into the same space, making the ecology richer.

Perhaps most significantly, the permanent grass and clover walking strips between and around the beds keep the soil fauna healthy and erosion to the minimum regardless of the weather. Such things are tremendously important.

Not so long ago all farms produced food out of soil, water, air and warmth because there was life. Nature charged nothing for her part.

Now we have absurd quantities of petroleum and natural gas going into food production, leaving an eroded, salty, toxic wasteland behind. We should know better, despite the propaganda of our twin "big brothers" of government and industry.

Basics

The most basic rule is balance. We have to strike a balance between opposite polarities, heaven and earth, silica and lime, grass and clover, bee and earthworm, give and take. This also means a balance between people, plants, animals, microbes and minerals. With balanced crops and livestock, rhythms and activities build up momentum within the farm organism. This rule implies that the greater the diversity the greater the health and stability of the farm. That is something to think about.

In the past few years hundreds of CSAs have come into being across America. It is an idea whose time has come. A few bits of land here and there are turning into healthy farms again. Wealth, made at the expense of the countryside, needs to be returned. Given half a century we may no longer be able to find corn to the horizon in a toxic cloud.

We have a choice.

Appendix I

Here are current addresses for some of the main "characters" in this story.

Acres U.S.A.
PO Box 91299, Austin, Texas 78709
(512) 892-4400, (512) 892-4448 fax
website: www.acresusa.com
e-mail: info@acresusa.com

Agronics, Inc. (fossil humus)
7100 Second St. NW, Suite E
Albuquerque, New Mexico 87107
(505) 761-1454, (505) 761-1458 fax
website: www.agronicsinc.com
e-mail: linvent@aol.com

A&L Plains Labs
PO Box 1590
Lubbock, Texas 79408
(806) 763-4278, (806) 763-2762 fax
website: www.al-labs-plains.com

American Society of Dowsers
PO Box 24
Danville, Vermont 05828
(802) 684-3417, (802) 684-2565 fax
website: www.dowsers.org
e-mail: asd@dowsers.org

Anthroposophic Press/Steiner Books
PO Box 960
Herndon, Virginia 20172
(703) 661-1594,(703) 661-1501 fax
website: www.steinerbooks.org
e-mail: service@steinerbooks.org

Anthroposophical Society in America
1923 Geddes Avenue
Ann Arbor, Michigan 48104
(734) 662-9355,(734) 662-1727 fax
website: www.anthroposophy.org
e-mail: info@anthroposophy.org

Biodynamic Farming & Gardening Association
25844 Butler Road
Junction City, Oregon 97448
(888) 516-7797, (541) 998-0106 fax
website: www.biodynamics.com
e-mail: info@biodynamics.com

Demeter Association, Inc.
PO Box 1390
Philomath, Oregon 97370
(541) 929-7148
website: www.demeter-usa.org
e-mail: jim@demeter-usa.org

Fletcher Sims (Compost Corp)
21400 FM 2590
Canyon, Texas 79015
(806) 655-4515, (806) 655-3022 fax
e-mail: compcorp@clearwire.net

Josephine Porter Institute of Applied Biodynamics (BD preps)
PO Box 133
Woolwine, Virginia 24185
(276) 930-2463
(276) 930-2475 fax
website: www.jpibiodynamics.org
e-mail: info@jpibiodynamics.org

Pike Agri-Lab Supplies, Inc. (refractometer)
PO Box 67
Jay, Maine 04239
(207) 897-9267, (207) 897-9268 fax
website: www.pikeagri.com
e-mail: info@pikeagri.com

Woods End Research Laboratory (soil testing, BD lab)
PO Box 297
Mt. Vernon, Maine 04352
(800) 451-0337, (207) 293-2457
(207) 293-2488 fax
website: www.woodsend.org
e-mail: lab@woodsend.org

Appendix II

Creative Definition Procedure

The following questions or instructions are to be taken one at a time until each is fully handled and answered. The purpose of creative definition procedure is to assist the individual achieve linguistic integrity.

1. What does the word (or symbol) _____mean?

2. Tell me some things the word_____doesn't mean.

3. Tell me some things that the word_____can be used for. (to describe)

4. Tell me some things that the word_____can't be used for. (to describe)

5. Tell me what the word_____can be associated with. (connected with)

6. What does _____ involve?

7. What does _____ exclude?

8. What words, symbols or things can the word_____be differentiated from?

9. What is the word_____similar to?

10. What is the word_____different from, and in what way is it different?

11. Give me a deliberately misunderstood example (sentence) using the word_____.

12. Is there an earlier subject or are there earlier ideas that affect or influence your understanding of the word_____? If yes, what?

13. What prior assumptions or beliefs are necessary to understand the word_____?

14. What prior assumptions or beliefs are necessary to define or give meaning to the word_____?

15. What isn't necessary for you to understand the word_____?

16. What isn't necessary for you to use the word_____?

17. Exactly how could you effectively convey your understanding of _____to another?

18. How does your understanding of the word_____seem to you now?

In using creative definition procedure here are some pointers to follow.

Use a good dictionary, preferably an unabridged.

It is often best to get a friend to ask you these questions and write down your answers, while you devote yourself to answering the questions fully, with reality and with as much truth as you can. Also, remember that if you are the one delivering the questions and writing down the answers, be attentive and open-minded, acknowledging all answers without invalidation, evaluation or advice.

Acknowledgements

I would like to acknowledge some of the people whose help led, either directly or indirectly, to the publication of this book.

Foremost my mother, Isabel, who mailed her last poem to me as I worked on this manuscript. She believed in my work and supported it when nobody else did. Then my father, Walter, as well as Peter Escher, Jack Horner, Galen Hieronymus, Hugh Courtney, Harvey Lisle and Vladimir Vanha, all key teachers. And, Charles Walters, publisher, who was willing to overlook my shortcomings as a writer because he considered my message important. Last, and by no means least, Thomas Carmichael, a tutorial editor whose extraordinary efforts to pare my verbosity and weld my scattered thoughts together may have made this book readable.

Index

Georgia authorities 168
Georgia driver's license 164
Gerdeman, Roger 150
German chamomile 110
gneiss 76
go along with the authorities 153
goat pens, chicken coops and fig trees 152
Goethe, Johann Wolfgang von 44, 51, 54, 95, 123
goethean 17
Golas, Thaddeus 36
gold 145
good 18, 27, 43, 44
good sense 157
good soil or rock powder 113
government agency 155
government research 65
governments tend to become corrupt 155
grain and legume covers 68
grains 58, 62, 62, 63
granite 47, 63, 73, 113
grass 18
grass and clover 186
grass, clover and herb clippings from around the beds 185
gravitational 53
gravitational polarity 49
gravity 15, 18, 49
grazed in rotation 89
greater the diversity the greater the health and stability 187
green onions, garlic, English peas, sugar snap peas 183
green revolution 139
greensand 71
groundhog 132
groundhog pepper 132

groundhog skin burned to ash 133
groundhogs 119
Grotzke, Heinz 41
GSR and repetitive processes 172
guarantor of deposits 179
gypsum 22
Hamaker, John 74
"hard-ball" researchers 65
hard clay 38
hardware cloth 18, 124
harmonics 30
Harvey Lisle 92, 97, 109, 110, 114, 118, 121, 124, 159
Hauschka, Rudolf 7
have you stopped beating your wife 158
head 53
head, heart and guts 31, 169
healthy BD farms 135
healthy farm 71
healthy root zone action 66
heart and circulation 109
heart, lungs and circulation 53
heaven and earth 186
hectare 1, 18
Heinlein, Robert A. 72, 180
Henshel, Julius 74
herbaceous 18
herbicides 66
herbiciding the dandelions 142
herbivorous 18
herbs 61, 181
Herzeele, Baron von 7
hide of the animal 131
Hieronymus, T. Galen 10, 27, 62, 104
Hieronymus instruments 189

levity 15, 21, 49
ley line grids 29
liberal 140
Libra, Aquarius and Gemini 54
Liebig, Justus von 42, 143
life and vitality 93
life ether 49
life force 21, 64
light 21
light ether 49
Lily Kolisko 19, 98, 101, 105, 110
lime 13, 22, 63, 71, 73, 74, 75, 113
lime and silica 93
limestone 73
Lincoln, Abraham 153
liquid 49
liver and the endocrine glands 112
loan to be paid at harvest time 151
local granite quarry 185
long range environmental improvement 149
long term goals 79
Louisiana hot sauce 182
Lovel, Hugh 165
low pH (high acidity) 73
machine 22
Magna Carta 146
magnesium 22, 73
magnetism 104
maintain a polite society 153
making BD 500 94
making BD 501 98
making BD 502 105
making BD 503 107
making BD 504 108
making BD 505 110
making BD 506 111
making BD 508 121

making BD Barrel Compost 122
making Homeopathic potencies 98
malathion 78
Malcolm X 153
man 102
manganese 74
manipulation of world commodity markets 138
manufacture and use of the BD preps 119
manure 37, 62
manure was too moist 124
manures 71
manuring 60
market garden 97
market research 66
Mars 7, 52, 54, 109, 113, 114
mass 174
mathematical duality 51
mathematical proof 87
mathematics 87
Matricaria chamomilla 107
matter 30
Mayan agriculture 119
Maxwell, James Clerk 49
McClintock, Barbara 117
McMasters, John 170
meadow horsetail 7, 47, 114
meat 181
mechanical 22
mechanical occultism 103, 104
medical associations 144
medical use of radionics 104
medicine 47
memorization 80
Mercury 6, 52, 54, 107, 114
Mercury was retrograde 126
Merlin 47

projective geometry 26, 50
proliferation of parasites 78
propaganda 150
propaganda techniques 147
proprietary knowledge 103
pro-social spending and
    anti-military 136
protoplasmic 75
proving self correct 176
psychologist/client
    relationship 172
psychology 66
PTO 26
PTO-driven manure spreader
    115
Ptolemy 3, 55
public and private debts grew
    152
public school 81
publishing or broadcasting to
    the masses 146
pulls nitrogen into the soil
    108
pumped up with his chin out
    166
pumpkin seeds 62
purification and excretion
    107
push planter 183
pyramids lending 137
qualitative 44
qualitative tests 74
quarry dust 61, 62, 74
quartz crystal 98
Quercus alba 110
Quercus robor 110
Quercus rubra 110
rabbit 62
rabbits 60
radar readout 161
radiant 49
radiant state 49
radionic 69

radionic analysis 74
radionic analysis and
    treatment device 134
radionic devices 27, 29
radionic reagent 129
radionic testing 78
radionics 23, 26, 30, 103
radish 39
ragweed 61
rainmaking 126
rainmaking ceremonies 112
rampant growth 121
rape 61, 62, 63
raspberries 37
rats 63
raw manure 38, 76, 77
raw material production 138
reaction to a stimulus 176
reading other people's minds
    175
real wealth 137
reality 27
realization 80
Reams, Carey 8
rear-bagging lawnmower 89
reasons for eliminating
    abundance 136
recipe for making barrel
    compost 122
recycling 180
red oak 110
reductionists 72
reexamining the specialist's
    view 154
referent 80
refined, balanced and
    harmonious
    relationships 93
refractometer 190
regenerative methods 29
Regulus 28
Reich, Wilhelm 24, 126,
    147

religion 27, 82
research 66
research and training
     institute 182
resemblances 19
resistance to tyranny and
     oppression 174
revenue for their town 157
reversal of the law of
     increasing entropy 147
Rhizobia 21, 27, 30
Rhizobium japonicum 61
rhubarb 37
rice 68
Rife, Royal R. 20, 147
rotations and interplanting
     186
Robin Hood 151
rock crushers 76
rock powders 68, 74, 113
Rodale, J. I. 23
Rodale Press 85
room and board 85
root burn 78
roots 53, 54
Roquefort cheese 182
rubber, 140
Russell, Bertrand 88
Russia 179
Russian 104
rye 59, 61, 62
rye and legumes 65
rye, vetch, turnips and rape
     89
Sagan, Carl 176
salts of nitrogen, phosphorus
     and potassium 143
Sarah 165, 166, 167
Saturn 7, 52, 54, 113, 114,
     121
savings and loan crisis 179
Savory, Alan 18
sawdust 37

sawmill bark 185
sawmills 37
schoolteacher 80
science 27, 82, 147
science, philosophy, religion
     and the arts 136
science, religion, philosophy,
     art and aesthetic
     endeavor 169
scuffle hoe 182
scythe 182
seaweed 71
seeds 60
seeds bred for response 183
seeker of wisdom 106
sensation and desire 93
sense 28
sense and desire 93
sensitive crystallization 110
sexual and metabolic
     organization 53
Shaklee 62
shape of the pile 113
shares 181
Shaw, George Bernard 65
shortage of games 17
shredded leaves 60
sidereal 25
sidereal astrology 4, 28
sidereal day 28
sidereal time 28
sidereal year 28
sidestepping provocation 165
significance 169
significance sphere 31
silica and lime 186
silica flour 98
silicic acid 10, 28, 99
silicon 74, 77
Sims, Fletcher, Jr. 9, 116,
     190
skeletal framework for the
     farm organism 111

skilled therapy 176
slavery and ruin 180
small intestines of a bovine 107
small is beautiful 136
smartweed 129
snap beans, corn, summer squash, tomatoes, okra 183
snap conclusions 87
snout 54
sociology 170
Soda, Ken 97
soil 29, 39, 60
soil fauna 66, 68, 69, 186
soil remineralizers 4
soil testing 190
solid 49
soluble nitrogen 77
sorghum cane 37
sorghum mills 37
South Africa 180
South America 140
southeast 65, 119
soybean/wheat rotation 67
soybeans 61, 62
space 29
specialization 141
speed trap 158
spiders 66
spinach 60, 61
spinach, lettuce and seasonal herbs 183
spiritual 29
spiritual human 31
spiritual reality 93
spiritual science 101
sprayed in the late afternoon 97
springtails 66
Sri Lanka 139
stabilizes nitrogen in manures 108

stable datum 80
stable society 135
stagger crops 185
stagnant atmospheric conditions 126
standard procedure in East Tennessee 164
starry background 54
Steffen, Bob 97
Steiner, Rudolf 1, 2, 30, 42, 45, 49, 52, 91, 101, 103
Stevens, Ms. 167-175
stinging nettle 6, 38, 47, 60, 108
stipend 85
stone circles 29, 95
stone grit 69
string theorists 29
strontium 90, 123
study 80
study and research 102
Stuttgart 105
sub-conscious emotion 79
subliminal cues 150
subsoil 40
subtle energies 29
subtle organic chemistry 72
succussing 25
succussion 19, 29
sugar 77
sugar plantations 140
sulfides 74
sulphur 74, 93, 107
summer/winter rotations 68
Sun 6, 28, 52, 54, 109, 114, 130
Sun is in Taurus 130
Sun, Moon and planets 54
sunflower seeds 60
superheros will emerge 1550
superior conjunction 131
superior root growth 66

Acres U.S.A. — books are just the beginning!

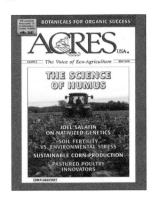